Foucault Against Himself

FOUCAULT
AGAINST HIMSELF

FRANÇOIS CAILLAT

FOREWORD BY

PAUL RABINOW

FEATURING

LEO BERSANI | GEORGES DIDI-HUMBERMAN | ARLETTE FARGE | GEOFFROY DE LAGASNERIE

TRANSLATED BY

DAVID HOMEL

ARSENAL PULP PRESS ◬ VANCOUVER

First published in French as *Foucault contre lui-même* under the direction of François Caillat ©
Presses Universitaires de France, 2014

ARSENAL PULP PRESS
Suite 202 – 211 East Georgia St.
Vancouver, BC V6A 1Z6
Canada
arsenalpulp.com

This book has been supported by the French Ministry of Foreign Affairs as part of the translation grant program. Cet ouvrage est soutenu au titre des programmes d'aide à la publication du
Ministère des Affaires étrangères.

Liberté • Égalité • Fraternité
RÉPUBLIQUE FRANÇAISE

The publisher gratefully acknowledges the support of the Government of Canada (through the
Canada Book Fund) and the Government of British Columbia (through the Book Publishing
Tax Credit) for its publishing activities.

Canada

Cover and frontispiece photos: "Michel Foucault at Home. Paris, 1978" by Martine Franck
(Cover: Magnum Photos PAR81742; frontispiece: Magnum Photos PAR1741)
Editing of translation by Brian Lam and Robert Ballantyne
Design by Gerilee McBride
Printed and bound in Canada

Library and Archives Canada Cataloguing in Publication:
Foucault contre lui-même. English
Foucault against himself / François Caillat ; foreword by Paul
Rabinow ; featuring Leo Bersani, Georges Didi-Humberman, Arlette
Farge, Geoffroy de Lagasnerie ; translated by David Homel.

Translation of: Foucault contre lui-même.
Includes bibliographical references and index.
Issued in print and electronic formats.
ISBN 978-1-55152-602-7 (paperback).—ISBN 978-1-55152-603-4 (epub)

1. Foucault, Michel, 1926-1984. I. Bersani, Leo, interviewer
II. Farge, Arlette, interviewer III. Homel, David, translator
IV. Rabinow, Paul, writer of foreword V. Didi-Huberman, Georges,
interviewer VI. Caillat, François, editor, interviewer VII. Lagasnerie,
Geoffroy de, interviewer VIII. Title.

B2430.F724F69613 2015   194   C2015-903473-6
                                            C2015-903474-4

CONTENTS

Paul Rabinow

Foucault Contra: No Laughing Matter?

During one of the interviews that Burt Dreyfus and I did with Michel Foucault—where we're asking him to be more precise, to align his terms better, to clarify his argument—he laughed (not his much-remarked-upon, haunted laugh from the underworld) with a certain joyous, unexpected grin and said, "I love America because when they claim to be asking me about the Enlightenment, they are actually asking me about the Enlightenment, something that would never happen in France. In Paris, it would be all traps and allusions and political references." How could one respond to that remark except with a timid smile? Was this statement in line with the common condescension of elite French visitors toward the happy natives of California, or a grin of release?

One of the recurring themes in Foucault's discussions

was how uncomfortable he felt, and had always felt, in France. He left his home country on many occasions (for Sweden, Germany, Poland, Brazil, Japan and, of course, often the US). This movement might be called flight from the strictures of bourgeois and petty bourgeois France. It might also be called deterritorialization from the normative, the settled, the already known, the given. Naturally, Foucault's trips registered a deep, and inescapable, ambivalence.

During 1980-81, I was an American in Paris. My flight and my deterritorialization were from the US and its academic fishbowls, to borrow a quip from Jean Genet, another peripatetic sort. If not thoroughly enamored with Paris, I liked being there. When I asked Foucault something about France, he would say, "I don't know as I never go out; you know France better than I." Of course, this confused and disoriented me. Although it was clearly sarcastic on one level, it expressed a kind of pathos, a mood and affect that Foucault would neither give into entirely nor abandon.

On the night of Francois Mitterand's election as the president of France in May of 1981, I arrived at Foucault's apartment at 7:50. The official election results were announced on state-run television at 8:00. Foucault already knew the results and was in one of the darkest moods I had ever encountered; he seemed close to despair. Later that night, a group of us went to the Bastille, where a joyous celebration for the victory of the socialists was taking place in the pouring rain. Suddenly a lightning flash illuminated the crowd, and just like that, Regis Debray—the dashing revolutionary and author made famous by his association with Che Guevara, who returned to France after his Latin adventures to pursue a career as a man of letters and leftist politics—appeared, and then shook Foucault's hand just as the skies lit up once again. Somehow with that flash of celestial enlightenment, our evening was over.

But Foucault's premonition that much more was growing dark proved all too prescient. His nasty and demeaning relations with the newly elected socialist government in France are well known. At the time, he was committed to the success of the Solidarity movement in Poland; the French socialist in power publically repudiated him and others. The minister of culture, Jack Lang, called Foucault a "clown." For a time, Foucault teamed up with Pierre Bourdieu to attempt a critical and committed response—but in vain.

From then on, Foucault's personal life in Paris drained him. He was living alone, traveling or dreaming about travel, and ultimately simply searching for a way forward. The novels of Hervé Guibert give us a tone of the scene without being journalistic reportage. It was decidedly bittersweet.

When he died in 1984, Michel Foucault left no will. In France, this meant that his estate passed to his mother and then to his family. Those who had accompanied him over the years were left nothing. Foucault's act has occasioned much discussion, although not in print; it caused deep hurt, although not in public. Foucault's motivation remains opaque. It is a scandal that has been covered over in almost Balzac-like terms. Like family scandals everywhere, but with a distinctive French cast, it has been buried but not necessarily put to rest.

With the family's approval (which took some time), the vast project of editing his published works as well as his lectures at the Collège de France was given shape. One must be eternally grateful for the care, scrupulous attention, vast labor and political acumen required to complete this project, even if the thirty years it took were not entirely exempt from a strategy to keep his name and fame alive as well as to establish who the legitimate inheritors were after all.

The recent, rather extravagant provincialism of Foucault commentary in France certainly qualifies as an example of Foucault (the author) contra Foucault (the man). We foreigners might well be accused of sour grapes over this not entirely accidental exclusion, but such an assignation would be false; after all, some voices, well established in their own right, and posing no interpretive risks to the Parisian orthodoxy, are solicited and welcomed by those who for the moment ordain what counts. It is comforting to recall Foucault's own discomfort and contempt for Parisian cliquishness and its inward-looking stance of superiority. The days when that stance was intimidating are long gone.

In 1966's *The Order of Things*, Foucault ended the chapter entitled "Man and His Doubles" as follows (English translation): "to all those who still wish to talk about man, about his reign or liberation ... to all those warped and twisted forms of reflection, we can only answer with a philosophic laugh, which means, to a certain extent, a silent one."[1] Actually, the original text in French is more cutting: "à *toutes ces formes de réflexion gauche et gauchies* ... "[2] A better translation of this devilish play on the word *gauche*, whose political meaning is "leftist," is "awkward and bumbling." Regardless, the laugh is a silent one.

Foucault was famous for his laugh. Actually, there were several laughs. Here, Jacques Lacan's theorem is telling: "*Le rire accueille la subjectivité prise au dépourvu*."[3] (Laughter greets the subject caught off-guard.) The haunted laugh from Hades might well have erupted when Foucault, having thought he had heard every form of baseness and deceit possible, was confronted by a new twist. There was another laugh, however, one seen more frequently abroad where the natives took his

---

1 Michel Foucault, *The Order of Things: An Archaeology of the Human Sciences*. No translator listed. New York: Random House, 1970, p. 343.

2 Michel Foucault, *Les Mots et les choses: une archéologie des sciences humaines*. Paris: Editions Gallimard, 1966, p. 354.

3 Jacques Lacan, "*La jeunesse de Gide*," Écrits, p. 763, Le Seuil, 1966, cited in Jean-Claude Milner, *Le Juif de savoir*, Paris: Grasset, 2006, p. 145.

work seriously, which meant engaging with it with unstinting admiration and questioning. At first, such discussion caught him "off-guard"; hence the new impish laughter of a surprising, animated *gai savoir*.

INTRODUCTION
François Caillat

Michel Foucault died in June of 1984. He left behind a body of work that has been published around the world, and is a source of inspiration for many thinkers, and the subject of a multitude of interpretations.

The man lived up to his work: he was a complex person with a number of apparent contradictions. He was a radical militant, yet a professor at the tradition-bound Collège de France; politically involved, yet a studious philosopher, happy living on the edge, though concerned with his central standing in well-known French institutions. He was a brilliant, incisive, iconoclastic figure. Speaking both in the classroom and in the street, he helped create the figure of the intellectual in tune with his times, using his personal experience to reflect on reality. He went far beyond his era and his country to become the authoritative thinker he is today.

Michel Foucault never sacrificed the gritty reality of his life for the world of ideas. The pathways he took display overflowing vitality and an appetite for constant renewal. We need to keep in mind the many facets of his life, from his arrival in Paris at the end of the 1940s, when the young man from the provinces began attending the highly-ranked École normale supérieure on the rue d'Ulm, to 1984, when the world-renowned thinker died of AIDS. These three-plus decades take us to university libraries in Sweden and Poland, revolt in Tunisia and student agitation at the Université de Vincennes in Paris, his classes at the prestigious Collège de France, and the fight alongside Jean-Paul Sartre and the French Maoists, not to mention American campuses, and gay enclaves in California.

Throughout his tumultuous existence, he built a methodology of thought, subject to variations and even refutation, moving from one discipline to the next, changing perspective and centers of interest, but always working in a coherent direction. Over thirty years, Michel Foucault's work traveled in different directions and took on different subjects, with an originality recognized by all and probably unequaled.

Foucault against Himself—or how a major twentieth-century thinker succeeded in avoiding any single definition of himself and his work.

∞

Four movements will help us understand who Foucault really was. They are like waves, or musical phrases. They situate the contrasting faces of the man and his work inside fertile relationships, and contribute to a portrait of incompletion, constant reevaluation, and adjustments orchestrated by Foucault himself. This perspective is not the result of a sudden decision or judgment made from without. These are movements that Foucault could easily be in tune with, and they confirm his taste for change and his rejection of certainty.

Variations on Power

The first movement concerns the question of power. The issue is central, not because Foucault makes it into a stated object of research, but because it keeps returning in different formulations. The question of power seems to outstrip his intentions by reappearing throughout his work and forcing itself on him. The issue persists.

"Variations on Power": this first movement applies to nearly all Foucault's works. We see how the issue of power is transformed, how it moves and takes on new forms through most of the research he did across disciplines, through philosophy, history, psychiatry, and prisons. There is no need to look at everything, since two of his books will serve the purpose: *Madness and Civilization* and *The Will to Knowledge*. In both works, Foucault renews his analysis of power, which includes turning it inside out and inverting it in its presuppositions and consequences.

In *Madness and Civilization*, which first appeared in French in 1961, the idea of exclusion holds sway. Power pushes aside, rejects, and marginalizes the different figures that denature social order: the mad, vagabonds, prostitutes, and homosexuals. Inaugurating the classical age, the "big imprisonment" displays the power of the negative, of darkness. A living part of society is suddenly silenced, excluded, forgotten behind its walls. In its decision-making function, power cuts off and separates.

Fifteen years later, in 1976, inclusion seems to inform *The Will to Knowledge*. Analyzing the role of sexuality in the West, Foucault describes, on the contrary, a kind of power with a positive aspect, the power to incite. It was apparently wrong to believe that sexuality was censored, repressed, and made taboo—instead, it was encouraged. Power does not forbid sex; it encourages its formulation via confession and admission, and it organizes constant speech and produces statements of truth. Power doesn't exclude; it constitutes.

From *Madness and Civilization* to *The Will to Knowledge*, Foucault changes his point of view and assigns new ways of functioning to the apparatuses of control. From one book to the other, the issue of power varies and returns in renewed fashion.

The Thinker and the Militant

A second movement, concerned with Foucault as a character, shows us that his agitation not only motivated his thought processes, but also touched on his everyday life as a philosopher, his concrete existence in society at a given time. We could choose the period between 1970 and 1975 in France to show that Foucault's personality was involved in divergent, sometimes contradictory activities. "The Thinker and the Militant" displays a Janus figure, a double-edged persona, a combination of reflection and activism.

Foucault is a thinker in his writings and in his role as a teacher, most notably at the Collège de France, where he started giving classes in 1971. In this temple dedicated to culture, a place where lofty minds met, Foucault worked alongside people known for their spirit of logical deliberation. But he did not project that smooth sort of self-image. He rejected the comfort his position offered and wanted to take his ideas to the street. Beginning in 1970 and 1971, Foucault supported Jean-Paul Sartre and far-left militant groups in their defense of immigrants and undocumented workers in their fight against deportation. Along with other intellectuals, he founded the Groupe d'information sur les prisons (the GIP, or Prison Information Group) with the aim of informing the public about conditions of detention and focusing media attention on prisoner revolts during 1971 and 1972. Foucault also got involved in the "Vérité-Justice" committees that were set up by the Maoists of the newspaper *La Cause du peuple* to denounce the everyday injustice of capitalism. He was not a militant in the organizational sense of the term, but he analyzed, wrote articles, and spoke up to explain and denounce. He took sides in political conflicts, but also when it came to events like the tragic fire at the 5-7 nightclub in Grenoble, or the Bruay-en-Artois murder in 1972. Foucault wanted to think about the present in the present, and get involved in current events, basing his thought in the political and social reality of the times. In this critical perspective, he was joined by the politicized intellectuals of the era, notably Jean-Paul Sartre (though they had strong disagreements about philosophy) and Gilles Deleuze.

Both thinker and militant, Foucault brought together these two ways of involvement in the world. He defended the concept of the "specific intellectual" acting at a given time and place, involved in short-term, sometimes minor problems, and calling for a localized response. These particular problems did not always require a generalized mobilization of the mind, nor did they demand the involvement of the "total intellectual"—the kind of intellectual Sartre referred to, who lifted the smallest conflicts to the level of pure concept. Foucault's position is based on circumstances. There's a taste for the present in his thought that completed or contradicted the outmoded image some people have of the thinker. By setting himself in the midst of events, with their unpredictable side and unexpected turns, Foucault ran the risk of throwing himself off balance, taking wrong positions, contradicting himself, and having to start all over or "unbind himself," as he liked to put it—free himself anew. But that seemed to suit him just fine. He insisted on living in the world's disorderly movement, and his own.

Where Does the Individual Fit In?

We can find Foucault's interest in the unbinding of the self in a third approach oriented toward man. The human issue—or, more rightly, the subject—arises in his thinking in a way that at times seems contradictory. We see, for example, how things change between *The Order of Things*, published in French in 1966, and *The Use of Pleasure* and *The Care of the Self*, his last texts published in French in 1984.

Of the first work, when it was published, people said it displayed a structuralist position and theorized about "the death of man" announced by Nietzsche in the previous century. His analyses of the different epistemological systems that have followed each other since the Renaissance in the areas of language, the body, and the economy are indeed compatible with the structuralist current that occupied the Paris scene in the 1960s. When the book came out, Foucault was stingingly attacked by the upholders of the philosophy of the subject and humanist thought; in this work, they saw the equivalent of what Claude Lévi-Strauss was doing in anthropology, Roman Jakobson in linguistics, and Jacques Lacan in psychiatry. Jean-Paul Sartre also weighed in against the book that he judged inapt to reflect on history and human lives; he described its author as "the last rampart of the bourgeoisie"—which didn't prevent the two intellectuals from working together ten years later in far-left groups.

Sartre's critique interests us because it points to the disappearance of a knowing subject in Foucault. After all, what place could it have once the structures of knowledge, which are unconscious and collective, have dispensed man from any thought or action, any voluntary creation, any mastery of the practice of thought? In *The Order of Things*, man is a subject constructed by culture, educated and educator both, measured by the yardstick of his times. Foucault broke with the classical theory of the subject as creator of thought. On the contrary: he considered man as an invention of history, born in the nineteenth century and already slated for disappearance.

Then, less than twenty years later, Foucault seemed to make a radical departure from this book that had launched so much debate. In *The Use of Pleasure* and *The Care of the Self*, he described man during Greco-Roman times who resembles, if not a creative subject, at least a being who creates himself via modes of subjectivity. Certainly, the man of whom Foucault spoke is not the knowing subject of classical philosophy, nor the subject, master of his destiny, the way humanist thought dreamed of. But here is a being of flesh and blood, sensation and thought, and Foucault wanted to describe the choices, pre-occupations, and active care he applied to himself. In this work on Antiquity, Foucault returned man to a central place in his reflection. He went on to build a way of being and thinking about relations with other people, a form of involvement in the social world, all things that could apply to any of us today. This new issue would occupy him until his death in 1984.

Over those two decades, his thought seems to have totally turned on its head, leaving readers of the time perplexed and at sea. In this change, if not a complete contradiction, there is a readjustment that once again displays the thinker's right to mobility of the highest order.

A Life on the Edge, A Job at the Center

The fourth and final movement describes the opposing positions Foucault occupied over a period of thirty years. He led a double life, pulled in two directions, a marginal being, far from society's norms, yet very close to the seat of power.

On one hand, "a life on the edge" reveals the progress of a timid young man from the provinces, wearing the straitjacket of his family background, rejected by the intellectual environment of the École normale supérieure, feeling excluded by the great difficulty he experienced in accepting his homosexuality, attempting suicide and sojourning in psychiatric hospitals, and deciding late to live out the rest of his life with great panache, far past the edges of social and moral order. All the ingredients for a life of passion were there.

At the same time, Foucault was careful to maintain a choice location in the mechanisms that produced and distributed knowledge. His pathway was exemplary, paved with excellence, following the elite road in France: the Henri IV Lycée, the École normale supérieure, the Collège de France. He didn't turn up his nose on prestige positions that placed him at the heart of institutions of knowledge and language: cultural attaché overseas, chargé de missions for various ministries, and jury member for the ENA public administration school in Strasburg. He exercised a vigilant eye as his works were published by the most powerful houses, like Gallimard and le Seuil. He succeeded in living a paradoxical and atypical life, both on the edge and at the center of a very standardized world. He drove a Jaguar and dropped LSD on a regular basis, and spent his days at the National Library and the National Archives. He hit the gay S&M bars in Paris as well as in San Francisco a few hours after giving a lecture in front of an audience of stiff-necked academics. He practiced excess to perfection, both in his intelligence and knowledge as well as the organized disorder and flaming out of his life.

In this very open game between private life and public office, Foucault danced a subversive *pas de deux*. Where others may have been careful or remained in outright rebellion, he decided not to choose. He proved that a person could be part of the seraglio but not transmit its customs. He showed how to develop personal freedom without becoming marginal. His freedom and refusal to maintain appearances caused some astonishment at the time, just as his death from AIDS caused a scandal. It was a sign of his moral and intellectual independence. Foucault never stopped reinventing himself and throwing off disturbing and contrary images of who he was.

∞

These four movements, among all the other possibilities, provide us with a confrontation of contraries, a staging of variables. This skewed perspective is true to Foucault's wishes. The thinker demanded the right to move about and to change. He refused to consider his works over and definitively finished; he preferred to speak of use rather than a body of work. He did not want his life, private and public, to be reduced to a single identity, and in the process risk turning it into something useful for policing.

Foucault against Himself: the way he wanted to be, the way he thought, against himself.

ON THE PERCEPTION OF THE INTOLERABLE
Arlette Farge

—You met Foucault after the events of May 1968.

Arlette Farge: I first became acquainted with him through his work in 1975, when *Discipline and Punish* came out. Back then I was a teacher for young educators who wanted to work in the penitentiary system, so I knew a lot about what Michel Foucault was discussing, and the way, for example, he would go into prisons to read *Discipline and Punish* out loud to the prisoners.

I admired him. Back then, street demonstrations, anything concerning freedom, utopia, the prison system, happiness, life that's intolerable—those things were objects of personal and intellectual interest for me.

—*What did you think of his social involvement?*

Arlette Farge: For me, everything began after 1968. I had returned to France after spending two years in the United States, where I had been part of a number of feminist movements, so important figures taking to the streets didn't surprise me. On the contrary—they encouraged me. At the time, it felt as if something was happening on a worldwide scale, so I was completely ready not only to accept, but to be part of it. But not in my professional life; I was still too young. I wasn't with the CNRS social research group yet. And I wasn't living in Paris but I participated from the suburbs, since I couldn't get to Paris because of the strikes.

—*Who was it that took to the streets? Foucault the intellectual, or Foucault the militant?*

Arlette Farge: He was a militant, that much was true, and he explained why; he spoke of the role of the "specific intellectual" as he would call it later, a subject he wrote about. I don't separate his trade as an intellectual from his work and social involvement. Everything followed a line of social action.

—Are intellectuals prescient about what will occur in society?

Arlette Farge: No, I don't think so. I think they support social change if such is their desire and if opinion is ready to accept them. Intellectuals don't gaze down on society from above. They support what they feel they need to. We feel something in public opinion and reflect on what action is necessary, then we take those actions. Foucault never wanted his words to be handed down from on high. I think he was a particular kind of intellectual who moved in solitary fashion toward the hot topics and conflicts of his times (madness, the prison system, the body, knowledge and truth) while reflecting on how the institutional game could be turned on its head and made to produce new places for knowledge.

—How did his discourse take shape? It's difficult to imagine.

Arlette Farge: I don't think the exercise was so difficult, since the prison system was so important to him. He traveled to Fleury-Mérogis and La Santé to speak with prisoners because he felt concerned about the darker side of society that cried out to be reimagined, and freed of academic ways of study and positivism. When you're completely convinced of something, it's simple and easy to get it across. But if you're standing behind a barricade of books, it's hard. But of course, he wasn't like that.

—*Was Foucault's way of communicating different from Sartre's, since they often stood in opposition?*

Arlette Farge: Of course, it was very different. Sartre's political involvement was much more generalized. He could talk about everything, any subject, in the press. Foucault didn't speak out in the press very often in the 1970s. Later, he would become more vocal.

—*Yet Foucault was an abstract thinker who pondered big philosophical questions.*

Arlette Farge: That's true, and that's where his ability to communicate was so strong. He knew how to place himself at the right level.

Getting back to the subject of prisons, *Discipline and Punish* is a masterwork that supports people who live behind bars, and even if they don't understand everything, they do understand that someone is coming to talk about them, someone is seeking them out to tell them that their situation is intolerable. For me, that's what a militant is, that's what a specific intellectual is.

—Discipline and Punish *came out on 1975, and the Groupe d'information sur les prisons dates back to 1971. In the book, do we find the ways of thinking he developed from his work as a militant?*

Arlette Farge: I'm not sure we can find anything that comes from his experience as a militant in *Discipline and Punish*. Foucault began a process of reflection in this book and that reflection spilled into other areas, which was emblematic of what his thinking would be later on. It would go on to serve subjects other than prisons, and move into the area of power and knowledge.

Of course, there are all the comparisons he made with colleges, the military and factories, which were adopted immediately by militant graffiti artists ("School = Prison").

—*Foucault never stopped moving from the local to the global and using specific cases to produce more general analyses of how society functions.*

Arlette Farge: I think that any small-scale case, any moment of discourse, any strategy, any exchange of speech or even anonymous words had great significance for him. Foucault worked in extremely narrow areas. And he had to battle to get people to accept that these narrow areas have great influence over other fields of endeavor. Reducing and narrowing an area of study was like a laboratory for him. And that laboratory was where his reflection took place.

Already, in *Discipline and Punish*, there was a lot of *The Will to Knowledge* present. Even if we think that he reversed his positions, when we read the two books, we see there's a very strong and very coherent continuity and logic, though he remained a sly and crafty person who liked to hide, and he hid well.

—*His book* I, Pierre Rivière *is history at its most*—

Arlette Farge: At its most infinitely small.

—*There's a relation there too with the small and local, isn't that true?*

Arlette Farge: Of course, and that's where Foucault was probably most misunderstood and criticized. Because of works like *Discipline and Punish* and *The Will to Knowledge* that are quite abstract and difficult for some readers, he was much criticized for not having understood the individual, the singular person, the small event. But books like *Herculine Barbin* and *Pierre Rivière* and *Le Désordre des familles*—we wrote the last one together—prove that he was extraordinarily attached to the lives of people who were not only excluded by society, but had never been known or recognized.

I often saw him in the archives, though historians criticized him for not having researched and interpreted archival material. His interest in archives was greater than any other historian's. He used to say that when he read certain texts like *I, Pierre Rivière* or the ones we worked on together at theBibliothèque de l'Arsenal, he felt a physical vibration. A physical vibration is more than an emotion; it's when your body begins to move and be moved. Intellectuals are often described as cerebral beings, but he was literally shaken at times. He said that he felt more tremors in the archives than when he read a piece of literary writing—and he read an enormous amount of literature. That's a side of Foucault people don't know. The emotional upset. He suffered because that side was never recognized.

—*That was his attraction for what Michon called miniscule lives and singular existences.*

Arlette Farge: Yes, because for him, a particular story was never just a particular story. It revealed much about the power apparatus that put people in direct contact with discipline and repression. Because these miniscule lives on which he worked at length could only be discovered through police archives—therefore, through a bias. What interested Foucault was this confrontation, and the resistance of isolated individuals who are confronted by power. I can personally attest to that, and the emotion that those people brought forth in him that no one ever understood. He was very hurt that no one recognized him for those works.

—*Because they seemed like a contradiction, or because no one wanted to see them?*

Arlette Farge: Because his way of writing in *Discipline and Punish* did not correspond to a historian's work. The historian works with files and quotations and standard footnotes. He creates bibliographies, and quotes the books he has worked on. *Discipline and Punish* exploded like a bomb in the world of historians. The book includes very few references, very few footnotes and, even worse, doesn't put forward a subject.

Very often, he would include expressions like "It was said that" or "It is not difficult to understand." That style was held against him and, during a debate that took place three or four years after *Discipline and Punish* came out, an assembly of historians, who had decided to finally look into what Foucault had written, accused him of being a bad historian. He countered the charges brilliantly, with devilish cunning and intelligence, because he could be devilish, and that possession that took hold of him was what made him so pleasant to be around.

—You mention the physical emotion because you spent time with him?

Arlette Farge: Because I wrote with him. How can I explain it? It was something that people around him, be they philosophers, intellectuals, scientists, and especially historians—since what Foucault wanted was to be recognized by historians—just didn't see. I'm not saying that they didn't want to see, but they saw nothing and heard nothing. Though it's true that when a philosopher barges into the historians' sandbox, some people have a hard time accepting the intrusion.

That was a time when the disciplines were very compartmentalized, and you weren't supposed to grab what was on someone else's plate. With *Discipline and Punish*, Foucault totally blew apart everything that had been said about prisons and the system of power.

Because that's the heart of the issue: disciplining the body, training it. Since I experienced it, I can tell you that he was not at all recognized for the work he did after that. For *I, Pierre Rivière*, a little. For that book, he decided to work with a team, including other historians. That was different. He published a very long text that accompanied the story. Then the book became a film by René Allio, a different object. This process was different from what we did with *Le Désordre des familles*: he went and sought out someone unknown to work with, me, and that certainly didn't help the cause.

—*He was criticized, but also very involved in universities.*

Arlette Farge: It was a rather unusual relationship because the people who attended his classes and filled the amphitheater of the Collège de France were not the usual university audience. They were very different; they were militants, and the way they dressed is worth noting. It would be interesting to look at photos because they really were the militants of their time.

They were coming to listen to a Collège de France professor, that's true, but for them he was both part of the institution and completely atypical, and he taught them something that went far beyond anything they had heard before. I don't know of any other equivalent. Even with Bourdieu. At the time, other professors at the Collège de France never had an audience like that: an audience of militants. I attended Lacan's seminars, and they were nothing like that. With Foucault, the audience was rapt.

His classes at the Collège were quite different from his books; they were very conversational. Foucault's conversational style was very interesting because it let him introduce all sorts of interstices, and he was able to slip all sorts of things through the cracks. He wasn't an institutional man in my opinion; he was bored silly by the prospect of having to give classes. He dreaded the whole process. He was afraid of it. Teaching was extremely hard on him.

—*Was the Collège de France a good place to take a stand?*

Arlette Farge: I couldn't say because I never spoke to him about what he expected from the Collège.

—*Sartre looked down on teaching in an institution. Does Foucault's relation to the Collège show his particular slant?*

Arlette Farge: Sartre is completely different. The extraordinary fame his books had, and his companion's as well; his is the story of a couple. Foucault is the story of one man.

—*Could we say that Foucault brought the margins into the heart of the most conservative institutions?*

Arlette Farge: Yes, and it was extraordinary how he turned his job at the Collège de France into something subversive. People always said that the audience there was made up of little old ladies wearing hats. And there are still plenty of them today. But in Foucault's classes, there were no little old ladies. To go and listen to Foucault was like proclaiming your desire for political change. But I couldn't say that he actually decided his classes would be like that, because I didn't know him enough on that particular point.

I never thought he was an institutional man. I never saw him that way, even in his personal reactions. I think back to 1981, when François Mitterand was elected president of France. Maybe I was actually there, since we were working together when he got a call from Mitterand asking him to accompany him to a celebration of his victory at a ceremony at the Panthéon. Foucault refused. In very clear and courteous fashion, of course. I didn't hear how Mitterand responded, but I did understand Foucault, that he turned down the offer because of his idea of the "specific intellectual." Of course, he had voted for Mitterand and he knew him, but he didn't want to be that sort of personage who appeared to be "in" with those in power and entering the Panthéon alongside the president.

—*It seems he introduced contradictions wherever he went.*

Arlette Farge: He always used to say, "I perceive the intolerable." I think we need to remember those words: "I perceive the intolerable." The further he advanced and the more he worked, the more he perceived the intolerable and the more he worked so it would be visible and others would feel it too. He also used to say, "I'll never be the same again."

There are two things about him. The first thing you have to know, and it's very simple, is that he really wanted to be recognized by historians. For him, history was something absolutely fundamental. And historians' indifference to him was quite painful. The second thing that was very, very special about him was his way of seeing the world. He could immediately and simultaneously bring together the greatest degree of abstraction with the universe of the private individual whom he met, or got close to; whose words he listened to.

—*He caused some outcry among historians, with his take on history.*

Arlette Farge: That's true. But remember that *Madness and Civilization*, which first came out in French in 1961, had a very hard time getting into print; a historian, Philippe Ariès, finally arranged for the book to be published with Plon. But remember also that Philippe Ariès was actually an industrialist and not an intellectual. That story is the beginning of something, and I think it's worth noting. First *Madness and Civilization*, then *The Birth of the Clinic*, and finally *Discipline and Punish* all had to come out before historians got into gear. As for *Madness and Civilization*, it's pure poetry. They could all see that. There is nothing extraordinarily subversive if you've studied a little history. But Foucault was a fox in the henhouse. Both amused and hurt. And happy to get his claws in there … Foucault was very strong on irony, very funny, very sarcastic, and always ready to kick at the wasps' nest.

But when his application to be director of the École des hautes études was refused because Fernand Braudel didn't want him, he was hurt very deeply. He would have been good there. He wouldn't have asked for the Collège de France if he'd been director at the École.

—*At the Collège, a chair was designed for him, made to measure.*

Arlette Farge: Sure, but there are a lot of chairs at the Collège that are made to measure.

—*Wouldn't you say there was a sort of mixture, a kind of impurity at the Collège compared to the usual traditions of French universities?*

Arlette Farge: I might not use the word "impurity." He shook up the ways people worked in the field of history, and that's never easy. I didn't know Foucault when I read *Discipline and Punish*. But I remember closing the book—I was working on the same subjects—and saying to myself, "Well, that's over, I'm finished working, there's nothing more to say." I spent a year assimilating that book. So I understand the historians' reaction.

At the same time, if you're a historian, you can't just stop. I had to find the energy to tell myself, "I'm still going to keep on with what I'm doing." That was before I finally met Foucault in 1980.

—*It was like a kick-start for you?*

Arlette Farge: The shock did me a world of good. As I said, I was practically in a state of shock due to his way of thinking.

There was something implicit in *Discipline and Punish*; people were asking, "What can we do?" And at the same time, he was doing something, he was acting, which challenged us a second time. But, intellectually, what could we do?

—How did you come to work with him?

Arlette Farge: The way it happened was totally improbable, a product of fortune. I got a letter from him. I'm almost afraid to say it, because there were very few books cited in *Discipline and Punish*, as I indicated, but my thesis was quoted. Everyone told me, "Look, he's citing you!" I couldn't quantify the importance of that. My thesis was about people who stole food in eighteenth-century Paris. In 1980, I got a letter from him, and then a phone call asking me to come and see him. I didn't know him. I didn't attend his seminars. I didn't go to his lectures. I was very intimidated. I hesitated. But then I went. To his house. That wasn't something you could refuse. He asked me, since I was working with archives that treated material similar to what he was working with—whether we could write something together, using the *lettres de cachet* and the requests from families to lock up their relatives. That was the end of my hesitations. He was extremely courteous, convincing, enthusiastic, funny, everything that makes the life of the mind so fascinating. That's how we started working together. In my life, there was a before and an after. A meeting like that will do it. Writing like that too, with him, for two years. I was the same, yet I was different.

—But you did know his work when he first contacted you.

Arlette Farge: Of course. I hadn't read *The Order of Things*, since I'm not a philosopher and it's difficult. But, of course, I knew him.

—So you wrote with him about the lettres de cachet. *Can you describe that?*

Arlette Farge: A *lettre de cachet* was an order by the king to have someone imprisoned. Normally, the king used them to push aside any higher-ups in society that he wanted to get rid of: disobedient aristocrats, for example. But, during a rather narrow period, from 1720 to 1750 more or less, an unusual situation occurred. Families from humble backgrounds began petitioning the king, appealing to him to imprison someone in their family. Maybe the husband wanted his wife locked up, or the wife—the system was egalitarian—wanted the husband put away, the parents versus the children or the other way around. These requests for imprisonment were completely exceptional since they occurred outside the law. Normally, when there is a family conflict, you have to appear before the police commissioner and justice is handed down. But in this case, members of the artisan class, often quite poor, went to see the letter-writer—because they didn't know how to write—to send a missive to the king: "This can't go on. My son is spending all my money." "My daughter is without morals." "My wife is a drunk." That sort of thing. And the king would or would not give his authorization to imprison the person. The files are thick—they are all held at the Bibliothèque de l'Arsenal—because all correspondence exchanged between the person imprisoned and the family, who sometimes expressed their regrets, was retained.

This material is absolutely fascinating because it is so ordinary. These are lives of no account. The everyday lives of people who are having family troubles, husbands and wives, violence and poverty, sexual misconduct, the little miseries of existence. That's what fascinated Foucault: what is the king doing there? What is the loftiest person who represents God on earth doing in this cesspool of poor people whom he never met, whom he disliked, his subjects with whom he wanted nothing to do?

We—I don't know if I should say "he" or "we"—were fascinated by the writings of these people that were presented in an oral style, since they were speaking through the voice of the letter-writer, and giving all the little details of their daily lives, and with the nerve to tell all that to the king because they wanted to escape normal justice, and at the same time be enlightened by the king. What we observed, and what was very moving, was the idea that they could touch the king. Without actually touching him, of course. But touch him all the same. Whereas the king touches you when you end up in a prison cell. But they felt they had touched him, and that's a very, very striking thing. Why did the king accept this? Why did he cast his eyes on these unformed pieces of paper? He did it over a period of thirty years. After that, there were so many petitions that he stopped, since his entourage began to grumble about the very principle of the *lettre de cachet*.

What I'm saying is that these family requests were unique. The esthetics interested us, the esthetics of these complaints, the esthetics of someone who had nothing to do with the king, yet who would ask, not for his justice, but for him to get interested in his case. The petitions were introduced with flowery terms of address that the letter-writer mastered perfectly, "For Your Majesty" and all that, and would end with a polite sign-off that had the subjects kneeling reverently. And, between the two, there was a swarm of poor nobodies who supposedly drank too much or did this or did that...

These perspectives, as well as the perception that we as

researchers were privy to people's lives during a specific period of the eighteenth century, represented for Foucault both an enigma, the enigma of power—what was it doing there?—and also a very, very strong sense of bringing these requests of humble folk to light.

That was the context when he talked about "physical vibration." And this rubbing up against power—that's the word he used—attempted by these unfortunate beings. That was something we shared very strongly.

—*That's what petitions do.*

Arlette Farge: And these were true petitions.

—*In terms of power, it's interesting.*

Arlette Farge: Of course. They were requests for repression. The suffering expressed is so great that they were asking for a family member to be moved out of the way. Afterward, there was no proof, and no justice. One thing that's interesting is to understand why, most of the time, the king agreed to the requests. From time to time he would ask for testimony from a priest to try and find out what was true. It was an example of repressive power striking a family, though it requested its application.

This was very interesting for Foucault. He said as much in *The Will to Knowledge* when he explained in very clear terms that when people, starting from a certain period, started talking about their sexuality and their faults, they began to confess and freely admit things. And in those requests, there were admissions. They were there. And that was long before *The Will to Knowledge*.

—Are these confessions about poverty and misfortune?

Arlette Farge: Poverty and misfortune, and petty, ordinary tragedy. That's what brought us together at those times: we shared a tragic vision of certain ways of life.

—Out of empathy or out of interest?

Arlette Farge: Out of a sense of ethics.

—Which means?

Arlette Farge: I have no taste for the tragic.

—*I meant interest in other people.*

Arlette Farge: Of course. Why would we be any other way?

—*You mentioned this "vibration" in the interest in other people.*

Arlette Farge: Yes, but later, in my life as a historian, I had no right to vibrations or emotions because I was a woman. That much I understood. So I'm careful. But how would a vibration prevent the intelligence from being moved? I'll never understand.

—*In this case you encountered a particular kind of sensibility.*

Arlette Farge: Of course. And it was completely unexpected. Improbable. Enough to make you wonder if it really happened, so improbable was it.

—*Did you experience that sort of exchange only with him?*

Arlette Farge: Michael Foucault also added very great intellectual rigor; we never remained at the level of emotional outpourings. Every wave of emotion was always transcribed with the goal of reflecting and questioning the emotion. If that hadn't happened, I don't think I would have liked working with someone who mixed his feelings into everything, since I never was like that. Perhaps the strongest thing was how we could transform all that into authentic knowledge, with his way of seeing things that was so much more advanced than mine.

—This book of interviews postulates Foucault as being against himself...

Arlette Farge: It's true, he was a man who liked to remake things all the time. On the other hand, I rarely witnessed any really deep contradictions in his work, except for one big one: the eight years of silence between *The Will to Knowledge* and his last books. There was *Le Désordre des familles*, but let's put that one aside. I saw his silence as that of someone wanting to question himself in some new, deeper way, and who would ultimately change his perspective in his last two books.

But maybe illness had changed his perspectives.

The main discontinuity, which for me remains a question— it comes as a contradiction with what he always said—is how he announced five books on the back cover of *The Will to Knowledge*, and they never came out, and the two that were published did not have the titles he promised. So something happened; I don't know what, and I wish I knew. For me it is the deepest question and the greatest contradiction.

What was his silence about? What self-questioning fed it? What dread? "Dread" was a word he used a lot. I often wondered about it. We were supposed to write a second book together. We talked about it often. But he didn't talk about his silence and I didn't dare ask him. For me, the greatest contradiction I experienced with him was his silence.

—What is dread, exactly?

Arlette Farge: Dread was something that belonged to him. It was one of his features. He worked with it, he worked on it … He thought about it a lot.

—How can we define it?

Arlette Farge: Dread can't be defined. Maybe it was the dread of the things he thought. Maybe his silence came from that, but that's just speculation. You'd have to ask his very closest friends, those who lived with him and were close to him. I was too far away to know, but I do know it was part of his makeup. Not fear on a daily basis. He wasn't afraid of getting hit by a car. Dread. There's something mystical about it.

—*To be seized upon?*

Arlette Farge: Absolutely.

—*What does Foucault's idea of "unbinding yourself," freeing yourself, mean?*

Arlette Farge: He meant it, on one hand, as never having ownership over what he said, what he communicated and, on the other, accepting the transformations that could occur afterward. Whether he accepted it well or badly. On a much deeper level, I think that unbinding yourself from yourself, for him, really meant abandoning or putting aside all that was most obvious. He often said that he worked on discontinuities of evidence. What historians considered obvious, such as linearity, for example, or continuity. He introduced discontinuity and break-offs. In his work, unbinding yourself meant freeing yourself from the academic nature of average endeavor: scientific, intellectually normal, historical, sociological…

A third answer would be this: unbinding himself, for him, was something very personal, it meant always being outside himself when he was indignant. There is a passage in *Discipline and Punish* about indignation: indignant, outside himself, the way we can be beside ourselves. But also outside the norm and outside stereotypes, rejecting everything that corresponds to the habits established long ago and that forces history to stay, like on a slowly flowing river, within the traditional boundaries of its banks leading from one spot to the next.

In response to Jacques Léonard—in *L'Impossible Prison*—who criticized him for his way of working, he would say that, in his opinion, a thought system, a power mechanism, an apparatus, were as much the subject as the subject itself. In his unbinding, many things were present. There was certainly something very personal and very ethical in his personality (never being where he was expected, being unbound from himself and surprised by himself), but there were also many discontinuities with traditional intellectual pathways that he came across every day.

—As in the break with some historians over the definition of what an event is?

Arlette Farge: His discontinuity with historians happened over his concept of the historical event. He very clearly stated that two things were important, in his view. First, chronology is not necessarily something that helps historians. Instead, he analyzed problems rather than successions of events that flowed together. For example, such-and-such riot led to revolution. For him, chronology is less important than certain apparatuses that arise at a given moment without there being continuity between the two, but that helped him reflect on what power is. He thought that what's real has its internal rules, an established apparatus, a system of thought...If a thing has already been thought, that doesn't guarantee its existence, but it does mean it's part of the history of what's real. That was extremely important for me in my work. What's real is not just what happens in facts. It's also what we think in order to reformulate things. It might not ever reach fruition, but this intellectual construction that certain philosophers and jurists of the time—people like Beccaria and Verri, philosophers like Diderot—thought of and perhaps never realized, that's part of what's real too. That's why Foucault fought the history of ideas. There is not one history of ideas and one history of the real: there is just history.

—*Foucault also broke with a number of norms when it came to the way he wrote.*

Arlette Farge: Michel Foucault's writing is magnificent. It's magnificent because it's contained, it's lyrical, it is as full of abstraction as it is metaphor. His writing is what touched me the most. Our encounter was built on it because I liked to write too. I wasn't looking to imitate him. He granted absolutely astonishing freedom to every historian and sociologist.

Today, I can see that freedom starting to work, and it makes me happy. In his writing, Foucault didn't let poetry run wild on the page. He integrated it into his intellectual reasoning, and the poetry fits into his text and turns his style into something beyond imitation. That makes for very beautiful reading. Not that it isn't difficult sometimes.

—*Did you pick up any hostility to his writing in academia?*

Arlette Farge: No.

—*Not at all?*

Arlette Farge: When it came to that point, there was unanimity. Everyone was surprised and blown away. People could contest him, but never his writing.

—He wanted to write the history of the dominated. Why was that?

Arlette Farge: I don't think we can separate an involvement from a choice of scientific object. No historian can say he or she doesn't have an intimate relation with his object of research. Maybe I'm wrong, but prison and madness, more than homosexuality—because of his work on medicine and the clinic—were his two very important focal points. They necessarily led to homosexuality because the medical knowledge that asserted that the homosexual is a madman and that the hysterical woman is a madwoman produced continuity. The focal point is exclusion. People don't talk enough about the magnificent book that I believe is one of his most beautiful, *The Birth of the Clinic*. Everything is there. The way the doctor gazes upon the body and the astonishing analysis Foucault gives us about the body and medical knowledge and anatomical dissection, the discovery of the body: everything he would go on to say or already said is in there. So, yes, the dominated. I think Foucault understood what it was to be dominated.

—In his view, violence organized the world by setting down borders?

Arlette Farge: Did he believe that violence is what organizes society? I would say that conflict with the many powers it contains forms its basis, but also the conflict with oneself, since these powers, as he explained so well, have all been interiorized. We are their bearers. We have power over them. The schema of power above and the people below—that's just not true. Foucault inverted the problem of domination—in the Marxist sense, I mean. I think what's important in his work is violence and power, how power is contaminated and internalized by all of us. That's where the strength of violence comes from. It enslaves us and sets us free.

LEARNING TO ESCAPE:
(MEDITATIONS ON RELATIONAL MODES)
Leo Bersani

—*Foucault first came to California in 1975. Did you meet him then?*

Leo Bersani: I first met him in Paris in 1974.

—*You were the one who invited him to California?*

Leo Bersani: Yes. I first came to Berkeley in 1974. I was asked to be the chair of the French Department, which was running out of gas at the time. Back then, the state of California had money, and the dean said to me, "Make this department into a major world class center of scholarship and thought. And invite whomever you want." The first person I thought of was Foucault. I wrote to him, then met him in Paris; we had dinner together and we agreed. He came the first time in 1975, then several times afterward.

—*Did people in the United States know who he was?*

Leo Bersani: Not really. He was known in the academic world, yes, but then something very unusual happened. Between his first visit in 1975 and his second one in 1981, he became quite famous. At the first public talk he gave in Berkeley, there weren't more than fifty people in the room. At the second, there was a crowd of two thousand. In the space of five or six years, something had happened.

—*French philosophy didn't have a very good reputation in the US in the 1970s. So inviting Foucault might have seemed daring at the time.*

Leo Bersani: Not at all. Actually, French philosophy had a very good reputation, but in a very small circle, not in philosophy but in literature departments, especially at Yale and Berkeley. Foucault was very well known among French literature professors, but also among those who taught English and Comparative Literature.

—*Were you able to introduce him to the Berkeley of the 1970s?*

Leo Bersani: Absolutely. I believe, during his first visit, Foucault discovered the new world of California. What was "new" about it was new for him, though it was also an important time in the history of California and America. Everyone is pretty much aware that it was a very great discovery for him. Not so much a discovery of academic life—he did his job well but that wasn't what interested him the most, I think—as the lifestyle he could observe in California.

—*Paris and California in the 1970s were like night and day. In Berkeley, the university was part of the real world, isn't that so?*

Leo Bersani: That's true. For Foucault, I believe there was a world of difference between the life he discovered in San Francisco, Berkeley, and California in general, and what he was acquainted with in France. That had mostly to do with the gay life in France at the time that was extremely uptight. For Foucault, that way of living was not very pleasant. It was absolutely the opposite in the California of the 1970s, the great era of the most liberated sexuality ever. This was just before AIDS, unfortunately, at the beginning of the 1980s, which more or less put a stop to all that.

—*You knew Foucault well. What was his relation to the institution of the university?*

Leo Bersani: I don't really know. The issue of institutions wasn't a problem for him, either in theory or in practice. We never talked about it. He did his work. He had excellent relations with his students. He very much appreciated being able to talk to them after class. I remember he liked to sit down at the table where he'd given his lecture and start discussions with them. That's what the institution was for him, I believe. And that's why, I think, he was much less happy at the Collège de France, despite the prestige, than at American universities where he could have that kind of contact. When I came to the Collège de France in 1982 or 1983, he told me, "What's really a shame here is that there's no exchange. You give your lecture, the audience applauds, then they go home." During certain seminars I could see—because he would express his frustration at the overly accepting silence of the students—him trying to establish a relationship with them, but it was laborious.

—*Weren't you surprised to see Foucault in a heavy institutional setting like the Collège?*

Leo Bersani: Yes, at the beginning. I was a little surprised to see him in this kind of setting because I had known him in a very different environment. Before every lecture, there was a little ceremony: you had to go through a special door, always the same one, and a porter from the Collège de France had to open that door so Foucault could enter. I found the ceremony amusing, but I'd seen the same thing in England, which is even worse. He went along with the ritual. He told me that was what you had to do, and he didn't protest.

—How did he relate his position to his personal life?

Leo Bersani: During his California period, I believe his personal life fed his intellectual life. Sometimes I found him a little naïve, but in a wonderful way. He often said—and it's an expression I myself use in my writing—that we needed to invent new relational modes. California revealed that to him. But it also stimulated his historical and philosophical production. What he was working at through his books, especially his polemic about sexuality in *The Will to Knowledge*, was a development of his discoveries of new relational modes. He wanted to pull us out of the regime, what he called the regime of desire, of psychoanalysis, of everything that defined sexuality for us, what it was supposed to be.

—By that, did he mean experiencing sexuality outside of what is imposed by psychoanalysis?

Leo Bersani: We first have to ask ourselves if the sexuality he was trying to speculate on outside of psychoanalysis is really an issue of sexuality. It's paradoxical: I believe he discovered the kinds of lifestyles that interested him through the sex life of the gay world. But at the same time, I believe it wasn't really sexual life that interested him. For example, when he talked about S&M practices in San Francisco, they opened up a kind of life for him that wasn't necessarily sexual. It was a certain way of being in relation to others that went far beyond sexual practices.

—These new relational modes were connected to friendship, correct? To the gay world, to sharing… But doesn't sadomasochism lead to more complicated relations?

Leo Bersani: Yes. Indeed, the relational modes he was thinking of were very complex. For example, when he talked about monosexuality, and of the way which not only communities of men but also communities of women could invent forms of friendship that were more difficult in the heterosexual world, he was getting to the heart of the question. Friendship between men and friendship between women interested him to a great degree. Once when I was giving a class on Foucault's texts, a woman student gave a very interesting oral presentation. She said that, in certain institutions Foucault studied, a friendship could be developed that wasn't sexual, but something else.

Do you remember that text where he writes, "Friendship ended … in the nineteenth century. We have forgotten what it is. We don't know the nature of friendship"? But there are examples of what that student called camaraderie, relations developed in the trenches, for example, during wartime; relations of great intimacy but that were not really friendship. Foucault discovered and wondered about all sorts of degrees of intimacy.

For me, the problem was this: how could S&M be at the basis of a discovery in which sexuality would be included in a new way of life? I've always thought that S&M—as much as I know about it—is a sort of repetition of normative gestures. In a certain way, there is a rather strict distinction between the dominant and the dominated partner. The pattern reproduces the hierarchical and power relations we find in the most conventional lifestyles. Foucault was aware of that, obviously. But for him, the interest lay in the reversibility of roles; the dominant partner on Tuesday could be the dominated on Friday. He thought that fact could even have an influence on so-called normal relations between men and women in which the man in general thinks he is the dominant one by nature.

The interest was not only a sexual one; it opened the way to the possibility of changing power relations between people, and especially between the sexes. There were also other more complicated things. He said, for example, that people who engaged in S&M had come upon completely new parts of the body that no one had ever discovered, and that were sources of pleasure. That claim intrigued me. One day I decided to inspect myself with minute attention, starting from my feet, and I didn't discover any place that was not already sadly familiar. I never understood what that could mean from the sexual point of view.

—*The* Use of Pleasure *and* The Care of the Self, *the works he completed shortly before he died, were looking into this issue. Is not the care of the self a search for oneself?*

Leo Bersani: Yes, I believe he was applying this idea of new ways of life to himself as well, and on certain very, very personal levels. I don't know exactly how. But I do know that the care of the self is an extremely interesting idea because, in Foucault's thought, there is often a mix of what seems to be an idea based mostly on sex, and other ideas that depart from a

certain elaboration of the self that includes sex but isn't necessarily sexual, a sort of art of living, as he himself said.

What does that actually mean? He gives examples from
antiquity, but it is very important to stress that what he meant
by the art of living refers to a kind of ascesis, a discipline that
aspired to pleasure. That's what's interesting. Discipline and
ascesis were not the opposite of pleasure for Foucault. What I
like most of all in his last works, especially the interviews, were
the ideas that were, so to speak, under-theorized, but that he
left as a legacy. One of those ideas is the difference between
desire and pleasure. I was never able to understand in what
way he imagined that we could have pleasure while eliminating desire. But I do know what he meant: it was by eliminating
the priority of desire in pleasure. Discovering or rediscovering
pleasure is a way of rediscovering sociality. Foucault did an
excellent job of sensitizing me to works, for example, in which
people try to rediscover a new form of intimacy through relations between bodies.

I'm thinking of two such works of art. There is Claire
Denis' wonderful film *Beau Travail*, where we see a sociality
among members of the French Foreign Legion that is not
homoerotic, but expressed through the choreography of the
military exercises she invented. In the second half of the film,
the members of the Legion perform exercises that are absolutely extraordinary; they aren't military exercises, but instead,

the choreography of relationships. In other words, how to work the body to make it engage in new relations with other bodies? There's a second thing that comes to mind, and I don't know if Foucault had an interest in it. These are the films by Éric Rohmer that often feature friendships between women who speak endlessly about love in the most conventional terms. These women, who have no other subject than men, are usually seated rather far from each other, and little by little they draw closer and end up kissing. Homosexuality has nothing to do with it. There's pleasure in the sensuality of language that ends up expressing itself through touch. That interests me to the highest degree. Gesture and touch are forms of pleasure that aren't centered on genital sex. When Foucault talked about his interest in S&M, I think he really meant degenitalization; it wasn't centered on the body's sexual parts, but could travel through the body as a whole. That's what takes place—not at all in a sadomasochistic context—in Claire Denis' film and in the works of Éric Rohmer.

— *Do you think* The Use of Pleasure *opens the way toward wider and more complete relations that go beyond desire?*

Leo Bersani: Yes, I do. We're not just redefining the way we "have" sex, as they say. It's also the way we live with other people.

Foucault was key for me when I started meditating, along with the British thinker Adam Phillips, on the idea of impersonal intimacy; that is, the development of relations with other people, intimate but not based on the curiosity and desire of others. I think that's what Foucault was criticizing when he talked about the regime of desire that asserts, "Tell me your desires, and I'll tell you your essence, who you are. What you desire is the equivalent of who you are."

You know that, politically, Foucault was subject to harsh criticism. In a famous article written by Edward Saïd, the great New York thinker of Palestinian background, he criticizes Foucault for getting involved only in "micro" political areas, not situated within larger questions. I think that Foucault responded to this critique in his seminars by saying that all truly revolutionary action must begin with a change in the relations between people. And that takes time. That kind of revolution doesn't need just two months or two years.

During my years of teaching, I never liked the activity. And when I retired, I actually discovered, as I began to give lectures here and there, that I liked teaching after all ... In a small group of ten or fifteen people, I discovered relations of impersonal intimacy. By that I mean we could speak of very important and very intimate things, but not at all on the level of the personalities of each member of the group.

—*To speak of intimate things without bringing your own personality to bear ... In your work you have often talked about Foucault's way of being there without being there, the strategies of avoidance he constantly used.*

Leo Bersani: Yes, he had a way of refusing to be assigned an identity. For years in the United States, in intellectual circles, "identity" was a negative word. There was no harsher criticism than to say of someone that he or she was doing identity work. The word doesn't seem very practical to me. I never asked myself, "What is my identity?" or, "What identity do I want?"

—*Foucault always fought the idea of closure. Could you feel that in the way he was?*

Leo Bersani: It was impossible to pin him down. But I found that just wonderful. There was something about him that would always escape you. He had this extraordinary way of laughing that was actually a way of dismissing himself, and going beyond what he had just said. A person can speak seriously without being serious, without taking himself or herself seriously, and Foucault had a wonderful way of applying something that Lacan, whom he didn't much appreciate, once said and that was completely in the Foucault style. During one of his seminars, he said to the young analysts listening to him, "If there's one thing I'm trying to teach you, it's to not take yourselves seriously." It's magnificent, an analyst saying that to people training to practice psychoanalysis. That idea of psychoanalysis would have pleased Foucault: to not be situatable, to be difficult to find. Identity is something we recognize. But with Foucault, we never got that feeling. I knew he took his ideas seriously, but at the same time, including with his students, he would always say, "No, you're not going to pin me down there." He was always experimenting with his identity as a construct. Does this identity suit me right now? Could this identity be useful politically? Could this identity help me sexually? I think that "identity mobility" is an absolutely crucial expression for Foucault—and for me as well, I must admit.

—To dismiss yourself... Foucault also spoke of "unbinding yourself," freeing yourself. Did you sense that with him?

Leo Bersani: I sensed that the idea of unbinding yourself from yourself was something he experienced. It wasn't just an idea; it was a way of being that people could feel. I also think it irritated a lot of them because he was so hard to locate. This had a strict relation to the idea of discipline. In order to function, a society of discipline needs to be able to find a person, locate him or her. Being there is another definition of identity.

So being fleeting was also a political way of not being definable by a name, an identity or certain ideas; everything that Bourdieu defined as the things that are expected of you if you have been assigned one type of social identity or another. How can a person avoid that happening? It's quite difficult. How can I be a professor without being one? I try and say to my students that the university should not be a center of knowledge, but a center of being. Learn to be fleeting rather than possessing a solid brand of knowledge. Students are always asking, "Do I have to put a lot of footnotes in the papers I write? Do I have to cite a lot of sources? Do I have to …?" I always tell them, "I haven't the slightest idea." When I write about an author, I never read the critics. I'm exaggerating a little, because I do read them, but only after I've finished my work. It's very important to be fleeting from an intellectual point of view. To unbind himself from himself—Foucault did that intellectually. The most notorious example is to have written the first volume of *The History of Sexuality*, and then decide that the history of sexuality could only become the history of the subject, the way in which Western society conceived of and formulated the notion of the human subject.

—*This way of changing wasn't new to him …*

Leo Bersani: I think Foucault's relationship with institutions was a given, but it provided him with a lot of freedom at the same time. He was a professor at the Collège de France, and that was an extremely strong identity in France, intellectually speaking. But at the same time, the fact that he was a professor there made him very famous elsewhere in the world. And so he was invited everywhere, to places where he could be this being who was completely different from how a Collège de France professor was identified. It was very useful to be a well known professor because he could play with that status. I'm not claiming he subverted the entire institution, but the institution became a point of departure for something fundamentally anti-institutional. And that's what's wonderful about the university: it lets you not be a professor.

—*Would you say that Foucault sought out positions at the center in order to live his life more easily in the margins of society?*

Leo Bersani: That is a very interesting way of putting it. I don't know if he ever formulated it that way, or if it was even a conscious intention, but that was certainly what he did.

Imagine, for example, that you are reading his last interviews, and you have no idea who he is. Then someone tells you, "He's a famous professor at the Collège de France." I think you'd be very surprised, given the great freedom of these interviews and their "underdeveloped" side. A Collège de France professor doesn't underdevelop...

—*Not to mention his lifestyle that alarmed some of his colleagues there...*

Leo Bersani: Of course. We have to return to that idea of Foucault trying to unbind himself. I don't think we can start imagining new forms of relations if we don't have this process of scattering the self, of unbinding the self's identity. Foucault tried to get Laplanche, whom he admired, into the Collège de France. That didn't work. When I asked him why, he told me, "He's too clear." That was a critique of the institution and, I believe, an indirect critique of Lacan.

One of Laplanche's interesting ideas is that the goal of therapy is not to bind you further. The person being analyzed is not a disintegrated being who comes to analysis to become more adapted, more coherent, more identified. Laplanche always said that the analyst's work is to un-do structures. I believe that's absolutely Foucault's manner. Analysis is, of course, a normative discipline that gives structure and adapts itself to social structures. But it's also a discipline of the taking apart of the self, and that's what Foucault wanted from himself. The discipline of taking apart: difficult to imagine, but essential.

—*Foucault died of AIDS. What was the reaction in the United States?*

Leo Bersani: I was in Paris when he died, and I was really shocked by the way the newspapers tried to deny his illness. In the United States, many people had died of AIDS. There was nothing more to say. It was horrible and that's that, there was nothing to add. What does it mean to interpret death from AIDS as a sign of the loss of a person's worth? I don't know what that might mean except as a horrible expression of homophobia. Maybe it was known that he was gay, but as always, society is willing to accept homosexuality as long as no sexuality is involved.

—*Foucault came to the United States to flee the norms of the time in France …*

Leo Bersani: That's true. The need to flee the norms in France is rather curious, since the great cultural cliché that dates back at least a century is that France is the country of sexuality. Actually, I've always found France rather puritanical. There are certain sexual behaviors that don't need to be examined. Your president can have a mistress and even have children with that mistress, and no one asks questions. That would be unthinkable in the United States. On the other hand, there is a sort of public acceptance in the US for things that the French reject. That's very paradoxical.

—*For Foucault, was San Francisco a way of escaping homophobia?*

Leo Bersani: I don't know. I don't remember if he spoke about it. Actually, I remember the opposite being true. There were aspects of university life involved with sexuality that he thought were strange. He used to say, "That would be inconceivable in France." That was back when the borders between students and teachers were starting to be defined. One day, we all received a letter from the university president—Foucault got one in his mailbox too—that informed the professors, "Here are twenty things you must never do with a student of either sex." There were all sorts of ridiculous things. Touching someone's hand, for example. That fascinated Foucault; he thought it was completely ridiculous and revealed a social and cultural way of being. He said that would never happen in

France. On the other hand, there was a kind of homophobia in France that didn't exist in the United States.

Foucault lived for a year in the middle of the gay neighborhood in San Francisco. There were also a lot of Eastern European families who had lived there for generations and they coexisted with no problems. There were any number of paradoxes, but San Francisco is the city that the rest of the US makes fun of for its freedom. Two or three months ago, a friend who lives in New York—a heterosexual—traveled to San Francisco. I asked him what it was like. He told me, "Oh, it's great. Of course I had to be careful because there are a lot of men who…" There's a built-in homophobia.

—*Did Foucault create conflicts within the university by bringing up sexuality, homosexuality, etc. in his books?*

Leo Bersani: I don't know if Foucault even thought he was in conflict with the university. He never said as much. The few things I remember about his life at the Collège de France led me to think he accepted it. I don't think he had a problem. The people who named him to prestigious positions knew what he wrote and what he was. At that level, it wasn't important.

—On the other hand, gay sociability is in part what allowed Foucault to build his university career, as Didier Eribon pointed out.

Leo Bersani: Gay sociability has always worked that way, in every milieu and every country. Just as there are circles and communities of men and women based on other common interests that end up playing a role in any advancement they may enjoy. It might appear unfair that certain types of sociability enter into the choice we make among people for a given position, but it's impossible to avoid. Foucault was aware of that.

—Foucault said that what was subversive about homosexuality was the gay lifestyle, rather than sexuality. But you criticized that idea ...

Leo Bersani: Yes. I had great hesitations about the idea according to which what scandalizes heteros about homosexuality is not the sex, but the lifestyle. It is true that there's a lifestyle. As I said, in San Francisco there was a world of sociability around homosexuality. I remember at the time, I said to Foucault, "I'm going to take you to a gay restaurant." Today, that would be just about impossible in San Francisco, or elsewhere, because there is a lot more integration. But that sort of thing did exist in the 1980s.

I think people found it a little strange, but completely

acceptable, that there is a homosexual sociability, that boys hold hands in the street the way Foucault saw them doing in the Castro. There is a famous sentence that says that when people see two men holding hands in the street, the idea that they just had sexual relations doesn't bother them, but their happiness does. They display a kind of happiness that homophobes can't tolerate. I don't agree with those words. I think the sexuality itself causes a problem for a large section of heterosexual society. The idea that a man would play the role of what they consider the woman's role in sexual relations, and that gay male sexuality includes very specific positions for a man's body that only women should adopt—that's intolerable for many men. It's also part of men's misogyny.

In his essay "Analysis Terminable and Interminable," one of the last things he wrote, Freud asserts that "the passive attitudes towards males" in men is one of the two "most powerful resistances" to analytic treatment. Not passivity with women, but with other men. He wasn't talking about sexuality in any specific way, but I find it fascinating that Freud said that it's the only thing we cannot overcome—that the therapist cannot cure. I believe that's the basis of homophobia. Respectability is the great payoff of marriage. As soon as sex enters the idea of marriage, marriage becomes intolerable. In the United States, we've all become well-behaved little boys. We get married, we all have wonderful relationships, and nobody talks about sex anymore. Sex has been relegated to the heteros. Hetero marriage has fallen into ruin. Now hetero husbands have other women or even other men here, there, and everywhere. The only respectable people are gays who want to marry, live in a straight neighborhood, and acquire all the characteristics of heteros. We have become society's moral conscience, the superego of hetero society.

—*How did Foucault place himself in relation to the political and sexual movements of his time? Did he support them?*

Leo Bersani: His critiques of sexuality in the first volume of *The History of Sexuality* were incompatible with censorship or the criticism of gay movements that were fighting for greater freedom in their sex lives.

I think he even mentioned it once in a conversation. He said, "It goes without saying." The fact that he fought against the privileged position of sex in the definition of the subject didn't keep him from believing that everyone had to acquire sexual freedom, as long as murder or non-consenting torture wasn't involved. In his view, S&M involved consenting behavior from both sides. He was against sexuality as a definition of identity, but he was for freedom—it was as simple as that.

KNOWING WHEN TO CUT

Georges Didi-Huberman

—How did you meet Michel Foucault?

Georges Didi-Huberman: I met him quite late. I am not a direct disciple of his. And I'm not someone who tries to meet the people he admires. I admired him very much, and still do. I read much of what he wrote. In 1981, I sent him my thesis on the pioneering French neurologist Jean-Martin Charcot—it's that simple—to thank him for his philosophical inspiration. He invited me to the Collège de France, and wanted to talk. It was magnificent, absolutely magnificent.

You know that Foucault was a philosopher who liked to laugh—that was an important thing about him. He liked to laugh out loud, and he smiled a lot. It was a sign of his generosity. And a very concrete sign of his generosity was this: he didn't take what was "general" in my work. He didn't agree with what was general in it. Overall, my work was psychoanalytic and, more to the point, inspired by Lacan. Foucault said to me, "It doesn't matter about all that." He took what was specific. And that was very generous of him. A dogmatic philosopher would have said, "You are following another line so we have nothing to say to each other." But he did the exact opposite. He went on to say, "What interests me is the work you did on Charcot's archives, the way you turned everything on its head." Because, actually, what I did, even if it was in line with psychoanalysis, really came from his book on the clinic, which is a magnificent work, a true masterpiece.

How can I sum it up simply? Foucault created relationships between practices and discourses, and I just added another element, images. Of course making images is also a practice. At the Salpêtrière Hospital, where Charcot worked and taught, image-making was developed to support a discourse that in itself was built on other practices. Everything was linked: discourse, practice, and images. Foucault was in full agreement with that point of view.

Then he said something to me that was extraordinary, and completely unexpected: he would have liked to have done a book about Charcot. But the director of the neurology clinic at the Salpêtrière—the hospital where Foucault later died—was also in charge of the Charcot archives, and he wouldn't give Foucault access. As a student, it was very clear to me how difficult it was to study Charcot as anything other than the inventor of the science of neurology, rather than someone who took enormous theoretical and practical risks, most notably regarding hypnosis and hysteria. Charcot went so far as to learn hypnosis with a carnival magnetizer, which is really extraordinary. Though Foucault couldn't carry out the research he wanted to in the way he desired, he was interested enough to keep all the documents I photocopied for him. And then, since Éditions Macula asked for it, he composed a truly magnificent recommendation letter for the Centre national du livre so I could publish my book with a grant for the reproduction of the photos.

—*What year was that?*

Georges Didi-Huberman: Our meeting must have been in 1981, as far as I can remember. The book came out in 1982, so it must have been a year or several months before publication.

I'd like to go back to the attention he paid. We could call it a kind of philosophical generosity, exactly the way Deleuze was. With both of them, if you weren't in agreement with any given aspect of their work, there was never a problem. As soon as there was a practical, specific point of contact with their work, the dialogue could begin. That's what non-dogmatic philosophy is, and it's extremely rare.

—Isn't that what occurred between Vuillemin and Foucault?

Georges Didi-Huberman: Yes. Exactly that. And even with Canguilhem to a certain extent. That approach wasn't completely limited to Foucault, but still, we know how the world of philosophy works with its compartments and exclusions.

—Foucault always wanted to avoid categories.

Georges Didi-Huberman: The first expression that comes to mind is "the gay science." And not only because of Nietzsche. Back when I was an undergraduate, if I have my dates right, Jacques Chancel invited Foucault to his radio show, *Radioscopie*. That made an impression on me. Chancel started in by saying something like, "Professor, you have so many degrees and diplomas, you know all there is to know …" And then Foucault interrupted him: "Okay, you can stop now. Diplomas are a form of social competition. Diplomas don't mean anything. Degrees don't mean anything. That's not how knowledge will be useful to us." There was a sort of ethics of knowledge in that statement and I felt very much at home with it; it was very important to hear that.

I'd like to talk about the first contact I had with Foucault. I must have been in my first year of philosophy and I had

François Dagognet as a teacher, which wasn't very easy. In Paris in the 1970s, everyone was reading Foucault. In Lyon, it was more complicated because of Dagognet. I started reading Foucault with a passion and I remember—this was another side to him—being swept away by the beauty of his language. He was an extraordinary writer. The proof? When I was trying to take notes on *The Archeology of Knowledge*, I practically recopied the whole book. I couldn't break his sentences. They were too beautiful to stop.

—Though his style evolved over the years.

Georges Didi-Huberman: Yes, but it was almost always beautiful. It was *written*. I think that art history is also a literary discipline. Even when you put together a catalogue, even when you establish a chronology, you make choices that are both theoretical and literary. They are literary because everything is written. Foucault, Derrida, and Deleuze knew that perfectly well: doing philosophy means writing because there are literary choices. There were other notable examples before Foucault: Bergson's writing style was very rich. Think of the opening of *The Birth of the Clinic*...extraordinary. It begins with a very short sentence about what will be investigated in the book: "This book is about space, about language, and about death; it is about the act of seeing, the gaze." The first sentence. And then immediately afterward—and it's a model for me—we literally dive into the heart of the matter: "Towards the middle of the eighteenth century, Pomme treated and cured a hysteric by making her take 'baths, ten or twelve hours a day, for ten whole months.' At the end of this treatment for the desiccation of the nervous system and the heat that sustained it, Pomme saw 'membranous tissues like pieces of damp parchment...peel away with some slight discomfort, and these were passed daily with the urine; the right ureter also peeled away and came out whole in the same way.' The same thing occurred with the intestines, which at another stage, 'peeled off their internal tunics, which we saw emerge from the rectum. The oesophagus, the arterial trachea, and the tongue also peeled in due course; and the patient had rejected different pieces either by vomiting or by expectoration.'"

The opening of the book displays a choice that is strategic, literary, and philosophical—in this case, a choice of immanence. The book is "about the act of seeing, the gaze," and then we are thrust into the object of the gaze. At the end of the book comes a realization that was very important for me: an act that is supposedly scientific, the clinic, is actually an esthetic practice, or at the very least, it has an esthetic dimension. Just as philosophy moves forward through literary choices, experimental scientific observation advances the same way, through the choices of the gaze.

—Foucault's writing was simple, yet he promotes reflection based on conflict, isn't that true?

Georges Didi-Huberman: Absolutely. The literary choice I'm referring to, which is so well illustrated by the beginning of *The Birth of the Clinic*, makes me think of Dante. It is so well thought out that at the end of each sentence, we say to ourselves, That's it, that's exactly it. And the beginning of the next sentence challenges what has gone before. This rhythmic kind of thinking—it's remarkable.

—Just when we think we've understood, he breaks down our certainty.

Georges Didi-Huberman: I'll add one more thing about his style: there's also something lyrical about his writing. It creates continuity in the literary gesture. Then there are all the effects of montage, which breaks down our certainty. It's plain to see. And no doubt it's inseparable from his fundamental decision concerning how he articulates a historical and philosophical issue.

What I'm saying might be banal, since everyone knows it. But, in practical terms, it's very hard to actually accomplish. It's so difficult that most of today's historians, including those at Les Annales history faculty, reject it. They have a lot of trouble combining the domains of history and philosophy. Today most historians will tell you that the study of history involves working without a philosophy of history, and without philosophy at all. Jacques Le Goff defended this position. Foucault believed the contrary. He is telling us, "The study of history means asking yourself philosophical questions." So writing philosophy means making literary choices. Studying history involves philosophical choices.

Faced with this constant difficulty ... that's what's so fascinating in his work. He finds the hidden problematic in every scrap of archive. So when the time comes to write history, we are absolutely not in the chronological telling of something, an episode or a period. What he is saying—and there's something of Benjamin here, though he did not see that—is that writing history is absolutely not a return toward the past, retracing our steps, thinking you are going to live once more in the cities of Antiquity. It's nothing like that. It means tracking the most urgent problems of today's world. It means working on that sort of archeology. When you do a dig, you are upsetting the ground of the present. You're upsetting the present, period.

Foucault also said something essential in his article about Nietzsche and genealogy: "Knowledge is made for cutting." I could work with that command (epistemic, but also literary, ethical, and political) for years. Making a documentary film means cutting. You'll have to cut the shot—and my words with it—at some point. Knowledge is knowing how to cut. Writing is knowing how to cut. And the high point is poetry, since we cut at the end of every line.

—*Let's go back to the relation between philosophy and history. It seems that Foucault's sport with the historians was not looked upon kindly.*

Georges Didi-Huberman: Yes, but in my opinion, it was less complex, insofar as there is a philosophical tradition of introducing historical elements. Hegel and Cassirer did it. I think Foucault knew Cassirer very well. The fact of being a philosopher, yet using historical material, arises from a well-established tradition, though less known in France than in Germany. Whereas, maybe I'm wrong, but it seems more difficult for historians to accept this way of stating the issue. You can see that there was never any problem for the reception of Foucault's philosophy, while today there's a problem with his reception among historians.

—*What is Foucault's relation to current thought today?*

Georges Didi-Huberman: In his article about genealogy, he makes a philological mistake, I believe. He says that Nietzsche didn't use the word *Ursprung*, or that it doesn't have much meaning. *Ursprung*: the origin. But we have to remember what Benjamin said about the word, which means "the original leap." In substance, Benjamin said that the origin is not the source of the river high up in the mountains. Origin is the whirlpool in the present at its moment of becoming. Nothing more, but the implications are enormous: the river is revolting against its own course. And that's exactly what Foucault calls "emergence" in that same article on genealogy. Foucault, who is very close to *Ursprung* according to Benjamin, was the first to get interested in these phenomena of emergence.

That's what fascinates me and keeps calling me back. When we work on images, of course, we are interested in the phenomena of *apparition*: what appears, what emerges, what suddenly comes to light. In the apparition—the emergence—we are constantly coming up against what we could call heterochronicities and anachronicities, which means that, in every emergence—say, the whirlpool in the river—there are pebbles brought down from the mountain, there is the state of the ground here, there is the configuration of the river at this given moment that suddenly changes the orientation of the current. We have different levels of time at the same moment, and the same spot (which makes space into something "heterotopic"), in the same event. That happens in every piece of discourse, and every scrap of archive Foucault analyzed.

Since the very beginning, I wanted to do with images what Foucault did so well with discourse. That means analyzing phenomena of emergence that have both long duration through time—which is why I refer to authors other than Foucault, to Aby Warburg, for example—and feature things that completely modify the current state of affairs and move toward the future. Hence the political aspect, which is fundamental. The political aspect in Foucault is completely linked to a movement toward the future, toward desire. Politics is what we do with our memory to produce desire, to produce something of the future, a possibility in our own practice.

—*Then emergence is unpredictable?*

Georges Didi-Huberman: There as well, I think there are possible complementarities between Foucault's positions and what Benjamin said about the readability of history. Suddenly, something of history becomes readable due to, perhaps, a particular moment in the present. A present moment makes something from the past readable for us. Foucault is at the heart of this issue. The meeting point could be Burckhardt, Nietzsche, and the entire theoretical tradition that culminates in Warburg.

—*But readability can't be taken for granted. Who is reading? Who can read?*

Georges Didi-Huberman: That's the question, isn't it? When you go to the archives, it's enormous, and you constantly have to make choices because you can't read everything. Foucault made choices; he cut. He made magnificent choices. He went places where, in the history of discourses, his predecessors didn't want to go.

This is one of the lessons in seeing: to look at what the sedimentation of previous discourses kept others from seeing. There are choices there too. And patience too, of course: working with archives is always very long and slow. And then suddenly something emerges—what do we do with it? And there I return to that fundamental idea: knowing how to cut. Cutting means both cutting in space and time, making decisions. A decision about knowledge. An ethical decision. A political decision. Which also begs the question, how do we organize knowledge? It's a question of method, in a way.

Concerning method, there is something that particularly

fascinates me in Foucault, and I feel I'm always working with it: the role of paintings in his work. For example, *Madness and Civilization* begins with a painting made by Frans Hals, if I remember rightly, *The Regentesses of the Old Men's Almshouse Haarlem*. *The Order of Things*, as everyone knows, begins with another great painting, the painting *par excellence*: Velázquez's *Las meninas*. Returning to *Madness and Civilization*, everything ends with another type of painting by another type of Spaniard: Goya. I'm interested in understanding what took place between Velázquez and Goya. I remember that magnificent passage where Foucault refers to another major representative of Hispanic culture, Borges. That's the famous list I call a "table." I make a distinction that Foucault probably did not specifically make, which is the difference between the painting and the table. Let's not forget that he was writing during the period known as structuralism when the notion of the painting as tableau was very useful. In *The Archeology of Knowledge*, he says something like, "Be careful. We know what a painting is: it's a series of series." So there is Velázquez, but there is also what people call the periodic table, where Mendeleev organized chemical elements according to their atomic number. And then there is Borges and Roussel... Order and disorder. Foucault is constantly moving between the two.

When you are working with images, you can't help but

enter that movement, that fine, splendid difficulty of the relation between order and disorder. Thanks to Foucault, we realize we can do something more than simply look at pictures and understand their mechanisms, which is the prototype of the structuralist way of working. We can do something beyond that, and see how the organizations of tabular images—what I call "atlases" in the manner of Aby Warburg—produce effects both of knowledge and of symptom in knowledge. Something that builds up and something that disturbs. Something that would be both Mendeleev and Borges. Foucault was between the two, of course, and that's what's fascinating.

—*So these are ways of combining?*

Georges Didi-Huberman: Yes. It's done through the act of cutting. When I say "cutting," I'm thinking of more exact things. I'm thinking of the fact that, when you're a historian or a philosopher, you create frames. There are millions of quotations in Foucault. But what is a quotation? It's a framework, a framework of sentences. Then, beyond the framework is the greater frame. What are you going to do with it? You are going to edit it. The issue of editing enters. It will make an enormous difference when it comes to the final product, depending on the choices we make, how we frame and how we edit. It's true for the cinema, and it's true when we're writing history or art history. Or even philosophy.

—*The reader cuts too, isn't that so?*

Georges Didi-Huberman: Yes: the writer as a reader and the reader as a writer. Foucault forced historians and philosophers to think about the issue of archives. He practiced archives. So do I. I worked on both the Charcot and Warburg archives. I haven't looked into thousands of them, but the taste for archives that Arlette Farge talks about, the smell of archives, I know about that. Practically as well as theoretically, what happens next is what Kant spoke of: *how do you orient yourself within thought?* For the historian, it's: How do you orient yourself within archives? Michel de Certeau asked the same question in extraordinary terms.

We create atlases to orient ourselves within thought. An atlas is not an archive. An archive is everything that people have decided to gather. It's an organization, of course. There are principles, and all the rest. The archive aims at totality, even if that's an illusion. I don't want to talk about Warburg too much in a conversation about Michel Foucault, but Warburg did create an atlas of images made up of some 1,000 pictures. A thousand images is nothing at all. In the life of an art historian, it's almost nothing at all. You can flip through a thousand images in ten minutes. Warburg has some 600,000 images in his photo collection So, to have created an atlas of 1,000 images means he really cut; he made choices and theoretical decisions.

This is a practical decision as well. Because when you have a thousand images, you have to organize them, the way Godard was able to do in his *Histoire(s) du cinéma*. There was an enormous amount of material, the history of cinema, the history of the twentieth century as a whole; so Godard cut, he chose, he edited. For all sorts of reasons: to remonstrate, to demonstrate, to elicit emotion. That's why the issue of cutting seems so important to me today, at a time when people think that knowledge means knowing the greatest number of things, as if databases were YouTube videos. That's very important, but the fundamental act is that of cutting.

Cutting doesn't have to mean reducing the meaning of something. Cutting is involved in the editing process. Through editing, we can open up meaning to include a considerable number of perspectives. It works that way with Foucault. He edits and opens up fields of possibilities. He starts with a very general idea—"This book...is about the act of seeing"—and immediately thrusts the reader into the experience of the doctor who is removing organic matter from a poor woman who has been immersed in a bathtub for a long period of time. There is considerable editing in that text. He chooses the scene with which he will begin. He tells it in magnificent fashion. So he's cutting. He comes out ahead on every level, including narrative. Readers can't put the book down. They make a choice and don't close the book or the meanings it carries. That's because he combined two things: "The act of seeing ..." and "Pomme treated and cured a hysteric." Really? What happens next? The questions begin. He achieved that through editing, and that's where the adventure and the history of the clinical gaze in the Western world begins. So cutting doesn't mean cutting things off. Not at all.

—*Actually, he's setting up a problem to be solved.*

Georges Didi-Huberman: That's it, a problem to address.

—*About closure, Foucault refused the term "body of work." He even disowned some of his books.*

Georges Didi-Huberman: On one hand he rejected closed systems, systems of dogma, yet at the same time he didn't seek refuge in subjectivity. Nor was there an appeal to the notion of the self-contained thinker, even if his language was as rich and beautiful as any contemporary writer's. He never said, "I am the center of what I am saying." Actually, there was a kind of modesty about him. Something about him, when we saw him in action, when we saw his evolution, made us understand that we were seeing someone at work. These weren't the opinions of Mr. Professor Foucault, the correct and true thoughts that Mr. Philosopher Foucault postulated. That would have been closer to Plato, or Dadiou nowadays; the one true opinion. That wasn't his style. Instead, he announced, I'm going to look, I'm going to observe this discourse, how it is organized; I'm also going to observe this practice, and ask the question about what produces the tension between this discourse and that practice. Set up a problem, in other words, starting from the differences.

—*Is that what sets truth apart from use?*

Georges Didi-Huberman: Yes; I think that, in Foucault, the concept of use is fundamental. But it's strange because, the more time goes by, the more analogies I find between certain of Benjamin's themes and Foucault's. In Benjamin, the issue of use is also fundamental.

—*Not to close things off. Always remain on the crest ...*

Georges Didi-Huberman: Absolutely. Not being a Foucault specialist, I couldn't say exactly how that works. It seems to me that there is no ontology of discourse with him. Not at all. But there is the observation of many discourses. I would say, without being absolutely certain, that there is no ontology of discourse with Foucault and that, in an almost mimetic fashion, I am trying to work with images without seeking their ontology.

I think, unfortunately, that was Barthes' temptation: to build an ontology of the image. But that doesn't work. We can say that Barthes failed on that point. It was a magnificent failure, of course, a striking failure, but it's a philosophical failure all the same. We don't build an ontology of images and we don't build an ontology of discourses. We observe, in history, the emergence of certain values based on use. We're observing something at work. Work in its very processes; its plans for immanence.

—*You're not a disciple of Foucault's, yet I hear echoes.*

Georges Didi-Huberman: No, I'm not a disciple of his insofar as there was no unilateral affiliation of "master" to disciple. But what about an art historian like myself who did studies on impressionism, the Renaissance and other such subjects, and who then decided to work on the photographic archives of an insane asylum, the Salpêtrière? You can see that one of the things that interested me from the beginning was the link between objects, "esthetic" practices, and epistemological issues. For that to take place, Foucault had to write *Madness and Civilization* and *The Birth of the Clinic*.

Two things struck me very strongly about the photos of the Salpêtrière hysterics: the subjects were beautiful women and, at the same time, they represented persons who were suffering. That was my problem at the start. There was an ethical issue that applied to every image, and it's the same problem that Foucault was addressing. I don't know if he would have put it in those terms when he analyzed institutional practices in different settings. An affiliation? Of course. But not a unilateral affiliation. It was no accident that, though I practically never send manuscripts to anyone, I wanted to send this initial one to Foucault. Even if I knew—let me repeat it—that there would be disagreement about psychoanalysis. In my opinion, Deleuze's and Foucault's position was much too reactive on that issue.

—I was thinking about a methodological relation between you and Foucault.

Georges Didi-Huberman: When I went to look at the Fra Angelico frescoes in Florence, I wouldn't have understood what I was seeing there, if I hadn't read Foucault; the art historical tradition hadn't seen it, and hadn't wanted to see it. I had to write two parallel books: one on the frescoes themselves and the other on a sort of historical epistemology of art history discourses that would explain why people had been unable to see this type of object, this type of emergence. I'm using the word "emergence" again; that comes from Foucault too.

That emergence had never been recognized, though it had been there since the fifteenth century. How could that happen? How did it end up breaking the barriers of one discourse and finding an existence in another kind? How is an object born? How is an object born that is both a historical and theoretical object? Foucault showed us exactly how that happens in the relation between the use of practices and the use of discourse.

—*Quite a few currents meet there.*

Georges Didi-Huberman: That's true. Except that, if we make the comparison with Aby Warburg, for example, Foucault worked more on units of time that are relatively short; several centuries. Whereas Warburg worked on periods of twelve or fifteen centuries, on the transmission and the "survival," as he called it, of extremely old motifs. For example, at the start of Warburg's *Atlas*, we see Mesopotamian objects that date from the seventeenth century BC, and their form is transmitted all the way to Italy at the beginning of the Christian era. Seventeen centuries! At the end of the atlas, we see photos of the concordat between Mussolini and Pope Pius XI in Rome in 1929, the theocratic and fascist event in action, with a political density—the very close relation of these images with European anti-Semitism—that runs through all it. Foucault was no doubt less sensitive to these enormous anachronisms. But that's normal since he was a contemporary of Lévi-Strauss, who had as a point of departure his opposition to Edward B. Tylor. Tylor's anthropology is one of "survivals" that was considered by the structuralists, justly on one hand and unjustly on the other, as outmoded and obsolete. But there are completely fascinating elements in these long-duration phenomena studied by Tylor. Foucault was not so much a historian of long durations, but he was one who set up the problems in discourses and saw all their strata. The way Arlette Farge does nowadays.

—*What do you think of the path Michel Foucault took?*

Georges Didi-Huberman: What surprises me most is how he

made it into the Collège de France. I'm saying that in relation to the state of disciplines that is perhaps more partitioned off today than at the time Foucault entered that institution. Where he was at his most remarkable, and where his lessons spoke to everyone and continue to speak, was how he showed us how to cross borders; to know territories, but to know how to be nomadic. In that way, he is close to Deleuze, of course: the Deleuze-Guattari tandem of *Mille Plateaux*, the "nomadic sciences" in opposition to the "royal sciences." Foucault was a complete nomad, and that's something magnificent. He succeeded in occupying a chair. But the chair was made to cross the borders of fields of study, the territorial fields of knowledge. That seems fundamental to me because fields of knowledge always tend to close in on themselves. Every small area of knowledge tries to become "royal," a royal science, a "sovereign" science. Even if it is small, this knowledge tries to become autonomous, with its own borders. Inside them, there is a king and there is expertise, and clerics. People could say to Foucault, "Actually, you're not an expert in Late Antiquity and theology ..." His constant transgression, his ability to pass and cross borders: that's what we have to use in today's world. It's fundamental.

I would also say that one of the characteristics of what we call an image is its ability to cross borders, walls, and other obstacles. Like a kind of ghost. Take the postage stamp, for example. A postage stamp is made to cross borders. Images, ideas, and the construction of fields of knowledge—if they turn into separate territories, they are going to end up having trouble. We need to deterritorialize their objects and deterritorialize ourselves. Foucault never stopped doing that.

—Is there a staging of intersections and encounters?

Georges Didi-Huberman: Yes, but again it's not a stage where his pleasure or personal fantasy is at play. I don't know what he would have said about that because it's not a usual reference with him, but it does seem to me that he took on Baudelaire's legacy, and what Baudelaire said about the imagination: knowing how to create relations between things that have no apparent link, creating "correspondences" and "analogies." That's how the imagination leads to authentic knowledge; the knowledge of unseen things. Maybe Foucault had problems with the unconscious, but in my opinion that's what it's about: when we say archeology, we're also saying the unconscious. When we create montages by crossing borders, when we place elements together that are not necessarily meant to be together, we are creating non-standard knowledge, and relations and relationships. We are creating them through montage, through editing, so either of two things can happen: the montage fails, it's gratuitous and leads to nothing, or we discover some fertile new analogy, something that reveals what has not yet been thought, and that makes what has been repressed rise up. That's the best-case scenario. That also concerns the unconscious; Walter Benjamin called it the optical unconscious. And Foucault often practiced it.

—So there's a great trust in the results of work.

Georges Didi-Huberman: There's trust, yes, but most of all risk. It begins as an improbable attempt. If we remain in the territory of expertise, we take fewer risks, that's for sure.

—Thought shifts in the same way wood ages over time…

Georges Didi-Huberman: Exactly. What I find extraordinary about Foucault is the way his work spoke. The idea wasn't to find out what Mr. Foucault thought. Of course, we knew what he believed in political terms, his literary choices and all the rest. But when he wrote, something was working on its own, independently; something heuristic, not dogmatic or axiomatic.

—*And his thought remains accessible.*

Georges Didi-Huberman: That's a side of his work that people criticized, the same way they criticized his friend Deleuze, or myself in the area of art history. But I think it's a very, very productive approach. The issue isn't whether we agree or disagree with something; the issue is whether the conceptual approach, the concept or question, can be productive, fertile or not. The concept of emergence I mentioned earlier is obviously productive. To say that knowledge is the art of cutting—that's productive too, even if it's not everything, even if it's not a complete definition of knowledge. And it doesn't really matter if it's the perfect formulation. It would be good to have one, certainly. But that doesn't mean it's a definition of knowledge. It means: This is what knowledge should do. What knowledge does.

—*Given those conditions, does Foucault have no illegitimate heir?*

Georges Didi-Huberman: It depends on how we define an heir. Is the heir the one who benefits from the will and what the will sets out? Or, in the case of someone who wrote books, are the heirs simply the readers? In this way, Foucault had thousands of heirs. We have to figure out what the effects of reading Foucault are. And we do know that he could be ill served when his work is presented in unhelpful ways. How is Foucault's Berkeley period presented today? What about his East Coast period? What is the Foucault of Université de Paris VIII or the Collège de France? There again, we are dealing with the value of different uses. We can begin to analyze the fate of discourses that claim a relation with Foucault. There are also many discourses that are heirs of Foucault's and don't even mention him by name.

—Foucault refused to admit to a fixed ideology.

Georges Didi-Huberman: When I first started reading Foucault, I didn't read him like someone who was in revolt. For example, his back and forth with Sartre completely went over my head. On the other hand, now I can see the interest in the polemical dimension of his work, which was something that repulsed me for years.

Doing art history, at the beginning, was like being immersed in countless beautiful pictures that offered consolation for everything else. Very quickly, the art historian gets disconnected from all sorts of urgent things, including the ones linked to theoretical battle lines and political debates. Foucault was a model when it came to this issue because he knew all about that problem, yet didn't hesitate when it came time to join in on the polemics. I'm aware of that aspect more now than I was at the time.

—*Could we say that Foucault's work is always political?*

Georges Didi-Huberman: Yes, totally. From the very first book, his action was political. When you question the organization of discourses or institutions, you're being political. I realized that long after my early years. I wrote a book that was published in 1990 in which I criticized the discourses of art history, in its historical aspect, from Vasari to Panofsky. A friend said to me, "You've written a political book!" I told him, "No, you're wrong, politics isn't my area. I don't know what it is." Now I think he was right. That understanding came to me through polemical discussions that I did not necessarily go looking for. When you are concerned with a cultural object, you're naturally in the political dimension, whether you know it or not.

—*About legacy, legitimate or not, how have people used Foucault? How have they managed it?*

Georges Didi-Huberman: I'm not a Foucault militant or a specialist, so I can't tell you. But what I can say is that we need to keep up our attention toward language: that way of not accepting certain uses of language. There are types of language that have to be criticized. The critique of discourses has to continue because new enemies are always springing up. For every era, we need a Klemperer or a Foucault.

—*You are a philosopher and an art historian. What did Foucault change in art history?*

Georges Didi-Huberman: What he wrote about Manet, for example, doesn't interest me. We could say the same thing about Freud. When he discusses a Leonardo da Vinci painting, he's not at his most fascinating. But when Freud looks at hysteria, he gives a veritable lesson in seeing.

I don't know why, but I always return to *The Birth of the Clinic*. When Foucault describes what the clinical gaze is, for me that's a basic lesson for art history. And also because he articulated the esthetic dimension in the broadest sense of the term—*aïsthesis*, or sensation, something that reaches us through our senses, the knowledge of the senses—as well as the construction of more theoretical bodies of knowledge, supposedly more scientific. He was ready to make the connection between the two. That was my experience too when I studied those famous photographs of the hysterics. Those women seemed to be the illustrations of a concept of hysteria created by Charcot's nosological discourse. Then I realized there was an echo with what Foucault was saying; it even, in some way, went a little beyond. Because these weren't only discourses. There was the fact of taking pictures at the Salpêtrière asylum that wasn't just an illustration of the concept or the discourse. There was the way the concept itself was formed and therefore, the practical dimension of the images had a crucial epistemological dimension. That's why I said that the challenge today is to do with images, which make up a large part of our environment, what Foucault did with discourses.

—*Don't these representations always come from dominant sectors in society?*

Georges Didi-Huberman: That might be an illusion created by the few illustrations in Foucault's books. There's the Frans Hals canvas: an official group portrait of bourgeois individuals. There's the Velázquez, a more-than-official group portrait, since it's of royalty. Foucault's disciples brought together these documents and called them *Archives de l'infamie*. I like that kind of research. It could even go a little further. Because the nameless—those *Namenlosen* whom Benjamin called the true objects and subjects of history—and the vanquished, however we call them, those who have no voices in the discourse:

they produce forms too. They produce discourses and bodies of knowledge.

It's up to us to leave our centers and discover these archives for ourselves, which is a lot more difficult. Take the example of *rebetiko* music in Greece. These songs are produced by Greeks who have moved within their own country: poor outsiders. In this music, there is an extraordinary mixture of different traditions (or survivals, or migrations) that gives birth to wonderful poetry that is completely political. It is an anarchic production from the most forsaken suburbs of Greek cities; a representation, but not at all official. The same goes for the *cante jondo.*

—*Can those representations reach us without a medium?*

Georges Didi-Huberman: Of course not. As Walter Benjamin said, we have to "organize pessimism" and in so doing, take on the theoretical and practical problems arising from technique. Sometimes there are people present to take notes, record, photograph, and film. Not always, but sometimes. There is enormous destruction, but survival too. At one point, the *rebetiko* gained some popularity; it was broadcast more often, there were recordings, and the words were written down or transcribed. That's one example. I'm saying this: we're wrong if we think that representation has to necessarily coexist with domination. People can represent themselves. At Tahrir Square, people did just that. They didn't need CNN to do it, even if their self-representation can't ignore the fact that CNN was there.

—*The survival of the fireflies ... There where power is found, so is resistance?*

Georges Didi-Huberman: I hope so. "Wherever there is power, there is resistance." That's not exactly what I said, but if you believe it ... It would be better if power were always accompanied by resistance.

—*Do you think so?*

Georges Didi-Huberman: If we're talking about Foucault, then we must both believe it. Yes, of course, I think so. The idea of fireflies is not so original, because that's what Deleuze, Guattari, and Foucault meant when they talked about the importance of the small. In Italian, a firefly means "a little light." A small light you can't completely see with full clarity. As soon as the spotlight is switched on, the firefly disappears. So you have to preserve the darkness, the night. There are minorities everywhere. Now they have to become active, even if it's in the darkness.

WHAT DOES IT MEAN TO THINK?

Geoffroy de Lagasnerie

—The issue that Foucault paid most attention to was power. Could we start there, with the notion of power in Madness and Civilization?

Geoffroy de Lagasnerie: We might think that *Madness and Civilization* is a book about the history of medicine, or the history of practices of internment and treatment of a certain number of individuals considered to be mad. But we could just as well read the book as a grand meditation on the theme of power and its functioning in contemporary societies. Foucault develops the idea that the essential operation of power is to produce borders, and divide society into two spaces: internal space on one hand, the space of things social, what is dignified and proper, the space of reason; and on the other hand, external space outside the world, space that belongs only to itself, dark and negative.

We then have to define what the normal world is, compared to this excluded space made up of groups of individuals assigned to positions of relegation. Power creates the exclusion between internal and external. Power separates, divides, and creates zones of darkness and shadow in society. *Madness and Civilization* is the history of these processes of exclusion, separation, segregation, and assigning a certain number of individuals to a zone outside the social world of "normalcy."

As well, *Madness and Civilization* takes on one of the themes essential to Foucault's thought: subjectivity in its relation to power. His very important idea is this: we must historicize what experience is. The experience of madness—people were not mad in the same way in the fifteenth century as in the eighteenth century, or the twentieth century—is historically constituted, and also constituted by the operations of power.

—*Foucault analyzed the banishment of madness in the seventeeth century. He called it the "classical event." There was rejection, yet isn't it true that asylums were established in the cities?*

Geoffroy de Lagasnerie: Power creates the Other and establishes a border between what is part of society and what is excluded. This can be translated by dispositions such as Descartes' exclusion of madmen from philosophical reasoning, or by internment in hospitals. What is important is not so much the place where the general hospital stands, but the existence of its walls. The building of walls—whether physical, architectural, mental, or disciplinary—means making a border in space and in people's minds into something material. This is the essential operation of power according to Foucault at that moment of his thinking. And that's why the asylum can be situated in a city: because certain individuals have been defined as Other, they can be interned inside the city. The more people have been defined as Other, the less uneasy we are at the thought of living with them, or near them; the less we are concerned by this neighborliness, since the border has been established between "them" and "us."

—For Foucault, is Pinel's liberation of the mad and psychiatry the same thing?

Geoffroy de Lagasnerie: The essential work of thinking is to uncover the mechanisms of power where they are hidden, where we can't see them. A certain number of ideas that were seen as liberating did, at certain times, have positive effects. I don't think Foucault would deny the existence of a liberating current in the new way of thinking about madness that Pinel helped bring forth, especially in relation to the old ways of treating the mad. But rather than accepting the word of psychiatrists, Foucault tried to see if they weren't just creating a new regime of power, a new manner of interning or designating the madman as Other, albeit with a more noble exterior; more humanist and more respectful of the dignity of the mad. Foucault's great ambition was to think of humanism as a new technique of power, and not the progressive liberation of people from the absurd constraints that once weighed upon them.

—*In the nineteenth century, the alienated became an object of study. What was behind this medicalization?*

Geoffroy de Lagasnerie: In reality, medicine is a product of the character of the madman such as he was constituted and isolated by institutional and legal mechanisms of discipline. Psychiatry flows from the birth of the character of the madman, whom it ratified as an object, such as he was produced by procedures of internment, control, and exclusion. What we call psychiatry is the recording of the construction of the character of the madman by procedures that are not medical. It is a science that receives its object of study from without. Foucault said, "Psychology will never be able to tell the truth about madness, since madness holds the truth about psychology." There is no reason why we began treating the mad with psychiatry, but on the other hand, we can question the birth of psychiatry as the ratification of the specific construction of the character of the madman in Western culture.

—*Are we talking about the distancing of the Other in order to make him into an object of study?*

Geoffroy de Lagasnerie: *Madness and Civilization* is also a history of psychiatry and, in a more general way, a history of the sciences that question the conditions surrounding the emergence of an object of knowledge. How did Western knowledge receive these objects and what types of divisions of reality allowed the existence of objects that could then be investigated? How do areas of knowledge emerge? The idea that there is something to know about a certain area—how is that idea born? In other words, how do objects of thought come into being?

The fundamental idea, I believe, not only in Foucault's *Madness and Civilization* but also in a certain number of his other writings, is that thought does not itself produce its own objects. He is fighting against the idea of an internal history of knowledge as something that can be perfected or that would liberate man through a supplement of awareness about himself. On the contrary: the origin of knowledge is impure. And this impure origin resides in the construction of objects that are the fruit of technologies of power that, in fact, isolates a certain number of entities, and separates them as specific objects that call for a particular science. The "scientific" perspective is not autonomous; it is preceded by operations of power that make it possible and provide it with its objects.

In this way, *Madness and Civilization* reconstitutes the creation of the character of the madman. Psychiatric knowledge will go on to seize this being and attempt to make a science out of him. Which does not mean that there is no psychiatric knowledge. Psychiatrists produce knowledge. But this knowledge is part of a power apparatus that reinforces it. According to Foucault, all knowledge in the social sciences is part of a power apparatus of one kind or another. To know is to control.

And that leads us to ask a question: how can we produce knowledge without the effects of control, but instead aim to produce the effects of liberation? This is the subject that preoccupied Foucault throughout his work.

—Would you say that psychiatry is a body of knowledge that can exist only within a certain exercise of power?

Geoffroy de Lagasnerie: In the classical tradition, when we think about knowledge, we always set it and its truth against the "political," against "vested" interests, the "normative," etc. One of the ways to disqualify a body of knowledge, or the idea that a statement or a proposition constitutes knowledge, is to argue that the statement or proposition is political, vested, or normative. The value of truth is associated with the value of the universal, the transhistorical, etc.

The very subtle idea that Foucault defends in *Madness and Civilization*, and then in *The Order of Things* and *The Will to Knowledge*, is that we can retain the idea that something is true—a body of knowledge—but at the same time accept that it's vested, historical, and political—in fact, because a body of knowledge presupposes a certain number of constructions of objects, and that these objects that call for us to study them are received by us from the outside, such as they were constituted by the procedures of power and control mechanisms. In this way, this is knowledge, but because we are dealing with knowledge, we know it is political knowledge. That's how Foucault can speak of a politics of truth.

— *With* The Will to Knowledge, *the question of power evolves, most notably in terms of exclusion.*

Geoffroy de Lagasnerie: As Didier Eribon pointed out, there is no "theory of power" in Foucault, so there's no sense trying to speculate about *the* theory of power in Foucault, the way it's too often done. Foucault never stopped changing his theory of power and even his definition of power. From *Madness and Civilization*, *The Order of Things* and *The Will to Knowledge*, and later, the various volumes of *The History of Sexuality*, we see a proliferation of methods and analytical frameworks.

It's true that there is considerable discontinuity between the vocabulary of *Madness and Civilization* and the rhetoric at work in *The Will to Knowledge*. I see two main points of discontinuity. The first concerns the question of whether society has a center. In other words, is there a place where power is situated, is there something that we can say organizes the social world as a whole?

In *Madness and Civilization*, we find the idea according to which the break-off between reason/unreason and reason/madness gives a vantage point not only on a history of madness, but also on a history of Western civilization. Beginning with one small object, we can reconstitute Western metaphysics as a whole, and Western history, by exposing the power that organizes and centralizes.

In *The Will to Knowledge*, on the contrary, power is a local thing, dispersed and heterogeneous; it is everywhere and comes from everywhere. So there is no longer any issue about a center of society born from a single fault line. Contrary to what was produced in *Madness and Civilization*, in *The Will to*

Knowledge Foucault does not turn the mechanism of sexuality into a point of entry that would allow us to see the dynamic at work in contemporary civilization as a whole.

We have this question: "Does society exist and does it have a center?" The answer is "Yes" in *Madness and Civilization* and "No" in *The Will to Knowledge*.

—What is the second point of discontinuity?

Geoffroy de Lagasnerie: The second sends us back to the question, "What does it mean to be the subject of power?" Or, this formulation: "What is the relation between the subject and power?" In *Madness and Civilization*, Foucault is stuck in a rather banal definition of power as a negative force. Power is what says No, what represses, what selects. The subject is therefore always constituted from without by a power that imposes borders of the forbidden, limitations and oppression.

But starting in the 1970s, and notably in *The Will to Knowledge*, Foucault develops an idea that is really quite beautiful and a lot subtler, according to which the subject is constituted by power. Power is not only, and perhaps not even mainly, a negative force that imposes constraints from the outside, but a positive force that creates and produces itself as a subject. To be subjected is the very thing that makes us exist as subjects. Power being a productive force, it is very difficult to free oneself from it and design a politics of opposition.

—*If we return to the first dimension, can we say that centrality comes from above?*

Geoffroy de Lagasnerie: I wouldn't say that in those terms. All of Foucault's studies are built around a very strong critique of the idea of the legal model, the idea according to which the State would be the place of power, an idea that flows from the liberal or classical bourgeois tradition. Foucault never asks the question of *who* is organizing. In his thought, we find no functionalism or study of intentions, such as wondering whether there was someone or some class that, at a given moment, wanted to produce the division between madness and reason. So I would not say that the fundamental break-off *comes from above*. The essential thing is not so much to discover where borders come from. Their existence is what matters: there is something in a society that can be thought of as a fundamental break-off. Here Foucault takes up a schema of Marxist thought, according to which a society does have a fundamental break. So if we wish to destabilize that society, we need only attack that border. Marxism defined that break as the economic system of class exploitation. In *Madness and Civilization*, the division between madness and reason present in institutions as a whole, and in people's minds, constitutes the basis on which the social world as we know it is built. If we attack that border, we destabilize the social world's functioning. In *The Will to Knowledge*, this idea is completely dismantled. The power relations are multiple, scattered everywhere, heterogeneous, contradictory. There is no fundamental struggle and society has no center.

—In The Will to Knowledge, *Foucault also criticizes the "transcendent" model of comprehending power.*

Geoffroy de Lagasnerie: One of Foucault's theoretical adversaries has always been political philosophy, Rousseauism and Kantism, what he called the legal conception of sovereignty. Foucault wanted to get rid of the idea that the State is the point of initiative from which power would flow down upon society. As I pointed out in my work *La Dernière Leçon de Michel Foucault*, one of his preoccupations was to break down the analytical framework of political philosophy—the notions of law, general will, etc., and the ways they prescribe how to think about the State as the site of power.

In the 1970s, when he began rethinking his model of power as a whole, Foucault reflected on this very particular manifestation called the *lettres de cachet* that allowed individuals to be incarcerated by order of the king. The *lettres de cachet* system is often seen as a sign of the sovereign's arbitrary power and an illustration of the idea of transcendence, power that flows down from above and governs the subjects. Foucault proposed another perception and developed a very striking idea. He asserted that these letters were not something that came from above. According to him, they were actually a kind of "public service." They were the sovereign's response to the proliferating demands rising up from below, a way of answering complaints and denunciations: "My cousin is behaving badly." "The lady next door is a drunk." "My father beats me." All this noise, this fog, this cloud of gossip and nastiness of everyday existence that is present tangentially, hovering in social life. So, in fact, power comes from below; it comes from the "people" and not from above. In my opinion, the issue of the places of power, and relations between power and the State and the space that the State should occupy in critical theory, represent essential questions today.

— *The idea that power comes from below, that would be a departure from* Madness and Civilization?

Geoffroy de Lagasnerie: I wouldn't put it exactly that way, because the State does not create madness.

—No, but it creates borders. Who builds the walls?

Geoffroy de Lagasnerie: The point is not to ask that question. There is no one there. It is simply done. It's like in *The Order of Things*. It is said but no one says it.

—But who makes the division?

Geoffroy de Lagasnerie: Just because we do something doesn't mean we're the initiators of what we do...

—No, but society produces it.

Geoffroy de Lagasnerie: But it's not someone, and it's not the State. That's the whole principle of the social sciences: things are done without there being a subject.

That's the whole difficulty of the relation with the social sciences, and what partly explains the resistance to a book like *The Order of Things*, one of Foucault's most beautiful books, but one that people sometimes tend to shunt aside with the excuse that it's a "difficult" work, and also more technical and less political and critical than *Madness and Civilization*, *Discipline and Punish*, or his books about sexuality. Yet *The Order of Things* is powered by a very important idea: against the notion—that is narcissistic—according to which society is aware of what it produces, and that there is a subject. Foucault shows that we have to write a history of the forms that began existing in a fashion completely independent of anyone who would have willed it, and that there are structured forms we can analyze and that completely escape anyone's decision-making, or any center or power.

—So there is an ongoing critique of intentionality?

Geoffroy de Lagasnerie: There is a critique, from the 1960s onward—from the time that *The Order of Things* came out— of all models of consciousness and intentionality, of the sub-ject and even, to put it in a more radical way, the idea that we must make the subject our field of study. In the 1980s, when Foucault began concentrating on the "processes of subjec-tivization," on subjectivity, on the relation of the self to the self, he was in a way regressing compared to the very radical move he made in *The Order of Things* when he wrote that the essential problem for thought was not subjects, but structured forms (of discourse, practice, etc.) which are not produced by anyone and are situated beyond any subject. These are struc-tured forms of thought that no one ever intended to think, but that are coherent all the same; there's a rationality to them, imposed on all thinking subjects of any given era. This manner of proceeding is founded on a disqualification of the notion of the subject and speech to the benefit of structured, historical forms that must be analyzed. That is a very, very radical departure.

—*In* The Will to Knowledge, *there is the notion of borders, and the notion of territory ...*

Geoffroy de Lagasnerie: The issue in *The Will to Knowledge* could be summed up this way: what does it mean to think that our sexuality defines us? Or, alternatively, exactly when did that curious and strange idea impose itself that, among the multiple things we do—among the dozens of actions we undertake in a lifetime, in a day—the very specific moment called sexuality is the center around which everything is organized that defines our truth as a subject? How was that incredible idea born that makes sex, the truth about sex and sexual practices, the basis of identity—or even, we could say, the operator of the construction of identity, that is, the idea of a stability of the subject through all its manifestations—in Western society?

—*How can we analyze* The Will to Knowledge *less from the point of view of sexuality and more from the point of view of power and psychiatry?*

Geoffroy de Lagasnerie: There is a whole domain of the Western world that maintains it knows something about sexuality. We call it psychiatry, psychology, and in its more modern forms, psychoanalysis.

Foucault often puts these three disciplines into the same category that he calls "the psychiatric function" or "the psychiatric discourse." They say they have knowledge about us, knowledge about the sexuality of individuals. Once again, what Foucault does is to say that, yes, it's true, they produce knowledge that is potentially very interesting about different types of practices. But again, the object of psychiatry is integrated into a very particular power apparatus that was born in the nineteenth century. It consisted, on one hand, of saying that an individual is not defined by what he or she does but by what he or she is, that individuals have a form of essence, that we are something other than what we do, that there is a form of permanence in ourselves throughout our actions; and, on the other hand, the center of this personality is sexuality. This new apparatus for the construction of characters, which is also an extremely strong principle of subjection, was ratified by psychiatry by making it an object of study and by producing knowledge about our sexuality.

—How would you synthesize the opposition between Madness and Civilization *and* The Will to Knowledge? *What do you think is the essential difference?*

Geoffroy de Lagasnerie: From *Madness and Civilization* to *The Will to Knowledge*, there is a major shift in the way societies are represented, and the image of the social world that is put forward. It revolves around this question: do societies have a center? In *Madness and Civilization*, Foucault asserts that the center of Western culture lies in the division between madness and reason, between reason and unreason, whereas, on the contrary, in *The Will to Knowledge*, he says that society is by its essence heterogeneous, scattered, power is everywhere and, whatever else, we must not believe that there is a center around which all realities revolve.

—To assert that power is everywhere is rather abstract…

Geoffroy de Lagasnerie: But what's much more abstract, it seems to me, is that power wouldn't be everywhere… The idea of a center, an essential division that would constitute the social world as a whole and that we could detect starting with the separation of madness and reason—now, that's a very strange idea. It's a magnificent intellectual construction, mind you, but very abstract.

On the other hand, we could ask ourselves why, before Foucault, no one tried to show, as he did in *The Will to Knowledge*, that power is everywhere. In every social relation, there is a power relationship. And power, for Foucault, is simply the existence of power relations. Someone wants to order my behavior, and I resist that ordering. That's called power.

—So is this power shared, mutual, exchanged, consensual?

Geoffroy de Lagasnerie: Power is the new name that Foucault gives to what we call social interactions or social relations. In any interaction, as soon as two people, two groups, come into contact, there is a power relation—therefore, there is power at play. Power is to be found in the most ordinary interactions of everyday life—buying a loaf of bread, saying hello to someone, borrowing a book. As soon as there is something like a social interaction, there is an apparatus, a framework, a system of behavior designed to prescribe what I should do. I am caught up in that apparatus and I try the best I can to resist it and carve out some freedom for myself.

—Could that be thought of as a definition of Marxism?

Geoffroy de Lagasnerie: Yes, but class struggle is only one of the means of production that power uses to take effect. In Marxism, class struggle absorbs all other struggles. Every struggle that emerges in the social world is perceived as being the incarnation or repetition of a more general struggle. There is never any singular power or singularity of power, since the same scene is being played out in daily life, in every struggle. The social world is a stage on which, at all times, the great story of class struggle between the proletariat and the bourgeoisie is being repeated.

On the other hand, what Foucault is trying to imagine is, if power is everywhere, then there is an infinity of struggles taking place at all times; though we might not see them, and some may be unconscious, each one is singular and specific. The role of the intellectual is to keep track of them, understand them, and encourage their proliferation.

—*Could we say that Foucault's thought is Marxism without class struggle?*

Geoffroy de Lagasnerie: Yes. We could put it that way. Marxism without class struggle. We could even say it better: a vision of society as warfare. Society is war: permanent war, war of all against all, war between individuals, war in sexuality, in the playgrounds and prisons, in daily life.

It's true, the idea of understanding societies by seeing them as warfare was a fundamental principle of Marxism. So we could say of Foucault that he built something like a form of Marxism without an economic model: a Marxism that doesn't tie struggles to the economy; that doesn't tie them to anything else but themselves; that liberates them. Actually, it's a fully developed Marxism.

—*There were a lot of shifts in Foucault's thinking. Would you say that he absolutely refused to build a dogma?*

Geoffroy de Lagasnerie: When you set all his works in front of you, a question immediately springs to mind: how can we imagine that the same person wrote all of them? It seems incredible that in twenty-five years—the period during which Foucault wrote—there could be so many styles, subjects, theses, and rhetorical forms that were so scattered, broken up, and incoherent. We could ask ourselves: what creates the unity of all these pieces besides the author's name? And what does "author" mean, since the relation between the books seems to come to nothing? The sense we get is very strong when we read several of Foucault's books in a row: is it the same author?

—He specifically sought out this fragmented way of being.

Geoffroy de Lagasnerie: The idea of a lack of cohesion, a way of thinking in constant contradiction with itself, that engages in self-revision and builds itself against its previous state to move toward the writing of future books—that's what Foucault simply calls writing. He says, "Writing means transforming yourself, unbinding or freeing yourself from yourself. If I knew where I was going, I wouldn't write." In the end, what matters is that the point of departure for each of his books involves freeing himself from the previous one. We could almost say that he is constantly writing against himself, in a dialogue with himself, insofar as he is starting out from where he had stopped earlier in order to become something else. That's why we get this feeling of complete incoherence, a breaking apart and loss of identity—unless we understand that his way of being consists of writing something new, and that writing itself can only mean writing something new, which involves discontinuity with what had been written before.

—You use the word "incoherent." Incoherent in relation to what?

Geoffroy de Lagasnerie: The dominant mode of thinking before Foucault was the construction of a system or discipline.

We set down a certain number of concepts and conceived of our work as a process of perfecting the concepts we'd established. Figures such as Althusser, Bourdieu, and Sartre represented this systematic kind of thought. That removes nothing from the greatness of their work, of course. Theirs was a very important way of proceeding, since it was based on an image of thinking as an assertion of a line of theory, a perception of the world.

Foucault's incoherence is in no way a failure of the system-form. It is a completely different concept of what thought is, wherein thought has value in itself. Each book has value in itself, it is its own experience, its own test. The next book could say something different, and it's not important whether there was a previous one. To call this idea incoherent would mean you were evaluating it by using the model of the system. It would be better to designate this path in some other way, based on the values of multiplicity and work.

—*In your book* Logique de la création, *you question whether there is even such a thing as a body of work in Foucault's case. You deconstruct the notion of the work.*

Geoffroy de Lagasnerie: It is difficult to speak of a body of work if by that we mean unity. At the same time, we have to remember that Foucault never stopped defining the principles that, according to him, organized his work. Every book's preface points this out: "What I wanted to do was this. In the next book it was something else and it wasn't at all the same thing." So, if you must, you can consider that there was a body of work in Foucault's case, but it's up to each of us to reflect on what constitutes it. One of the challenges it sets down is this: "You are my readers; tell me what my work is, and come up with a perception of my books yourselves. My work will then be simply the consequence of reading."

—Don't we run the risk of thinking only for the moment? If each book wipes away the previous, what guarantees each one's value?

Geoffroy de Lagasnerie: The fact that each book was conceived by Foucault as a separate experience and a debate in itself, paradoxically, doesn't mean that his books are actions situated in time and place, but instead, actions that have created a new present. Far from being limited to the moment of their creation—as if they spoke only of current events and Foucault's life at the time he was writing—they are books that build new perceptions and new theories that are unique each time. So instead of being relegated to the past once they are written, they open up a future for his readers.

In this way, every reader of his books can have the same experience that Foucault had as he wrote them, which included freeing himself from preexisting thought to see reality in a new way. And that experience is eternal.

—*So Foucault is less a thinker of his time and more a visionary?*

Geoffroy de Lagasnerie: Deleuze called Foucault a seer, someone who makes us see new things. In fact, the big problem with Foucault was one of visibility, the division of darkness and light. What do we see at any given time, how is it that we see what we see and, of course, what do we not see? That's what Deleuze means: Foucault is not abstract. It seems very difficult when he starts manipulating concepts, when he talks about psychiatry, language, and punishment. But, actually, Foucault's thinking is part of "life experience," the way we experience reality, the way we consider it, and see it. Each of his books offers a fresh pair of eyeglasses, a totally new light on reality; and we emerge from reading them as changed individuals.

—*But isn't Foucault very much part of his era?*

Geoffroy de Lagasnerie: One of the major questions in

Foucault's work, and maybe one of the essential inspirations of his thought, is: "What is the present?" That question has defined critical activity since the Enlightenment: what are the current affairs in which we are living? What does "today" mean? What we have is an image of philosophy that is almost close to journalism: how to understand the present. Foucault was guided by that idea and took his subjects from the conflicts he saw around him, the political and intellectual debates that were happening during any given period. But at the same time, the job of intellectuals is never to be the spokespersons for the present. The point is not for them to become amplifiers for a form of politics that existed before them, but to constitute new political objects.

The idea that madness is a political and not just a medical issue is something completely new, a new vision of things. Foucault was interested in the era's thinking around the asylum and the treatment of the mad. He chose his object from this political space, and from that decision, he built a new vision of the problem, and thereby, of our present.

—*He was also involved in very concrete activities.*

Geoffroy de Lagasnerie: There is a very strong connection between Foucault's practical, political involvement and his more conceptual creations. There is also what might appear as a tension between the involvements that seems completely local, a matter of circumstances, and a body of work that reflects on Western thought as a whole, on civilization, the world in its entirety, with its history.

The concrete involvement—passing out leaflets, supporting a refugee—is of course very important. But thinking, theorizing, reflecting—these are also essential activities in any drive toward liberation. Foucault dismissed the anti-intellectualism of struggle for struggle's sake. Thought is necessary too. But at the same time, the risk of reflection is that you can close in on yourself; thought becomes a game for its own purposes, an empty esthetic, complicit with its own concepts.

And from that flows the need to keep returning to the fields of action to fight alongside others, so you don't lose sight of the whole point of thinking, which is to free a prisoner, get papers for a refugee, raise workers' pay.

—*In* Madness and Civilization, *Foucault says that power silences people. In* The Will to Knowledge, *he says power makes them talk.*

Geoffroy de Lagasnerie: Like all of Foucault's books, *The Will to Knowledge* was born of certain struggles, and is part of the context of sexual liberation, Freudian Marxism and homosexual movements that were fighting sexual repression. Above all, it's a politically charged book that takes those discourses seriously, and joins the greater project of challenging the system of power that runs people's sex lives.

But for Foucault, being part of these struggles doesn't mean becoming their ideologue, but instead, radicalizing them: "Is the thing you want to liberate, which is sex, not the very thing you must liberate yourself from? Are you not the victims of the power you think you are denouncing? Is there not power also in what you are presenting as liberation?" Hence, the idea of a project that would look like this: "Of course we have to challenge the repression of sexuality, but perhaps the most radical project would be to free ourselves from sex."

—*He goes against intellectuals like Reich. Yet he's part of that same milieu.*

Geoffroy de Lagasnerie: In *The Will to Knowledge*, the logic of writing and argumentation leads him to say some very harsh things about Reich and the theories of sexual liberation according to which law and power and capitalism oppress our desires, and that by liberating desire we blow the system apart. Foucault was severe in his mockery of this ideology, but at the same time his intellectual undertaking was part of the context of a general rethinking of the place of sexuality in contemporary power apparatuses. We can consider his book both as a critique of Freudian Marxism and having sprung from Freudian Marxism, insofar as it asks: "How can we reflect on the relations between sex, power and modernity?" Foucault adds that the problem might not be stated correctly; perhaps it should be framed in another way. The role of the intellectual is to listen to the social conflicts coming to the forefront, and the ideologies that are circulating, and then radicalize them by proposing new ways of seeing sexuality in contemporary power structures.

—*Is that proposal Foucault's alone?*

Geoffroy de Lagasnerie: No. It's a position Foucault made his own. But it's also a general attitude that defines basically what an intellectual is. Figures like Sartre, Deleuze, Bourdieu, and Derrida and today, Didier Eribon and Judith Butler, all incarnate this way of thinking and engaging in theoretical activity in their relations to practice in the present day: an attention to emerging struggles, considering the problems they bring forward, and especially, *most of all*, never striving to serve any one struggle, but using them as points of departure to produce new theories of reality. I think Foucault, in that way, even if he does it with particular potency, takes up the figure of the intellectual that we know from Sartre. Between Sartre and Foucault—and even between Foucault and Bourdieu—there are many more resemblances than differences.

—*Foucault defined himself as a specific intellectual. What is a specific intellectual when compared to a total intellectual?*

Geoffroy de Lagasnerie: The reinvention of the theory of power that emerges in *The Will to Knowledge* involves a redefinition of politics, and of the figure of the intellectual. Once we agree that society has no center, and that power is everywhere, each struggle has value in itself. First of all, we should never believe that some struggles are more important than others—the struggle of transsexuals is as important as a strike in an auto plant—and second of all, we should not believe that every specific struggle is a particular incarnation of a more general struggle, as if, for example, every strike or mobilization repeated a grand, worldwide conflict. Each fight and each outcome must be understood in its singularity. We need to understand at all times what is at stake in an emerging conflict.

From that point on, the intellectual, Foucault asserts, "must become a specific intellectual." He can't believe, as Sartre did, that deep down, all struggles are fighting for the same values, as if the cause of refugees, homosexuals, workers, and blacks all referred to the same struggle for justice, truth, freedom, etc. As if politics were a stage on which we endlessly replay an eternal battle with different actors. Foucault says, "No, we're not going to build politics with universal values. We have to take hold of what's singular. At one given moment, the homosexual cause is at stake. At another given time, prisoners' rights are what's at stake, and that's something different. To understand things, and discover the specific problems in each struggle, we have to work, and the person who will work and produce knowledge about the struggle is the specific intellectual."

—Then what happens to the hierarchy of goals and battles?

Geoffroy de Lagasnerie: That's the most surprising and difficult idea to accept in Foucault's theory of power such as he developed it in the 1970s: no struggle is more important than any other; we must never think there is a political hierarchy, or a hierarchy of political temporalities that would lead us to declare, "This problem must be solved before that one." Or, "That involves only one individual, or a small minority; we have to concern ourselves with the majority." For Foucault, all struggles are central. Because everyone is the center of his or her own life, because social life is dispersed, there is no hierarchy in politics, all conflicts are equal and we must lead the fight and be vigilant at all times.

—*Could we say that the beginning of* The Will to Knowledge *is written against* Madness and Civilization *in terms of silence and speech?*

Geoffroy de Lagasnerie: *The Will to Knowledge* is not just a critique of theories of sexual liberation. It's also a critique of Foucault written by himself. That's why, of course, he's so harsh; we're always harshest with ourselves. After all, what he is denouncing in *The Will to Knowledge* is a concept of power as an apparatus that works to repress and prohibit, which leads to a concept of liberating politics as a tool to free different kinds of speech. Power as censorship and liberation as a freeing of words is exactly the analytical framework put forward in *Madness and Civilization* with the idea of the madman who is silenced—the madman incapable of speech and who, in any case, if he spoke, would speak nothing but madness, the absence of any work. In *Madness and Civilization*, Foucault was searching for those moments when madness erupted and temporarily escaped the walls: Nietzsche, Artaud, Bataille, and Van Gogh are examples. The idea of power as exclusion and speech as an act of resistance is totally canceled out in

The Will to Knowledge. Foucault is turning the critique against himself in order to rethink a theory of power beginning with questions of sexuality.

—*Does this also lead us to rethink power in relation to knowledge?*

Geoffroy de Lagasnerie: Beginning with *The Will to Knowledge*, talking, speaking your piece becomes an act prescribed by power. The totally exceptional idea in *The Will to Knowledge* is that power demands that we speak, it commands us to speak, whereas in the classical tradition, speech is what power fears. When people speak, publish, and print, power is on its guard. That's where censorship enters. We have always believed in the theme that power fears the word and wants to silence it. But in *The Will to Knowledge*, Foucault says, "That's what power does: it makes us talk, it asks us to talk and think that it's important to talk." That's a new concept of the relations between power, discourse, and speech, and it undermines the basis of *Madness and Civilization.*

We can see that this concept involves a redefinition of political action and the notion of resistance. If power censors and oppresses, then subversive political action takes the opposite form; it opposes repression by speaking up. But if power produces us as speaking subjects, then the art of resistance must take on a different shape. It's not enough to speak out in opposition. We need to displace the lines that have been set down. We need to create a politics of invention: invent other words, other ways of speaking, other subjects of speech, broadcast other subjectivities than those that power produces. In *The Will to Knowledge*, it's not enough to speak out to resist; we have to speak about something else in a new way.

—*What was Foucault's position toward the university?*

Geoffroy de Lagasnerie: To make it possible to create his work, Foucault broke with the institution of the university such as it was in the 1950s and 1960s. Foucault wasn't the only one. It was a general pattern among intellectuals that I pointed out in my book *Logique de la création*: to create, you need to free yourself from the image of thought as it was developed and imposed by the university.

When we look at intellectual fields of endeavor in the 1950s and 1960s—what I describe is true for the university in general—there are a certain number of subjects, references, and legitimate ways of writing that wholly predetermine the space of the thinkable and the speakable. Which implies, in a certain way, that there can be no new thoughts emerging from the university. But Foucault made it possible to produce new thoughts. How does one manage to produce what is forbidden? By producing new spaces. By reading avant-garde literature like Bataille, Klossowski, and Artaud, by immersing himself in the literary and social science journals of the time, by reading psychiatry, Foucault broke with the institutional references of 1950s-era philosophy, and by doing so opened the doors to producing innovative thought, the kind we can read in *Madness and Civilization,* though the process can be seen throughout his work. Finding new spaces, speaking to new audiences, discovering new partners to exchange with—this was what Foucault was always doing.

He didn't just write innovative books. He produced new spaces of thought and references that emerged and went on to help him to think in new ways. This radical autonomy—to be one's own founder—is in total discontinuity with the academic idea of discipline, profession, and research constituted and circumscribed within the institution.

—*Yet the beginning of Foucault's career was completely classical.*

Geoffroy de Lagasnerie: When we consider his progress, we are struck by the fact that he possessed all the legitimizing degrees and titles, yet at the same time, his practice was highly innovative and his objects of research totally illegitimate before he came along. On one hand, he attended the École normale supérieure, got his philosophy degree, and defended his thesis at the Sorbonne, which makes him look like the perfectly appropriate academic. On the other hand, he worked on writing history books, which for a philosopher was completely new. And not just any history, not that of some prestige object, but the history of madmen, then the history of prisoners, and next the history of sexuality. These were unworthy objects that he brought into the field of legitimacy. This contradiction is everywhere in his work and it is a fine one, since it illustrates his remarkable capacity to resist being tamed by institutions.

University institutions and others that form the elite like the École normale supérieure very often produce individuals who will conform to ideas of what is considered worthy of study. They want to raise themselves to the level of the institution that gave them their consecration, and so they choose the most conformist models, the most pompous writing styles, the most legitimate subjects, the most noble, since nobility cannot help but reproduce itself. Foucault managed to use the capital of the institution and its symbols to transform the definition of philosophy and the very activity of thinking. He used the institutions to redefine the field of the thinkable for everyone, rather than being tamed by them. That's one of his great contributions to contemporary thought.

—*Did his work at the Collège de France follow the same pattern?*

Geoffroy de Lagasnerie: Foucault completely understood that subverting and questioning the social, academic, symbolic, and political order comes from the center. He broke with the romanticism of the marginal. First, we can produce new definitions of philosophy and new radical ways of thinking only if we have nothing to prove to the institution, only if we're legitimate and legitimized by it. Once we have nothing more to prove, we can bring forward new objects without fear. The École normale supérieure, the philosophy degree, and then the Collège de France gave him the means to start building new ways of thinking and using the capital and the recognition as instruments to be even more radical in his thought and involvement in politics. Foucault put into practice the idea that only when we are in the center can we free ourselves of it.

—*Does that mean we should always keep one foot in the places of power?*

Geoffroy de Lagasnerie: There is no place that is outside power. There is no place that is outside of society. The strategic question we ask ourselves is not so much, "How to escape power?" but "What type of power can I use to expose the game played by a certain kind of power at a certain time?" In a way, what Foucault did by accumulating positions at the center of institutions, while retaining his marginal positions in politics, was to use symbolic and institutional power to denounce political power, and eventually academic censorship. He mustered a certain type of power against another type of power. That's what freedom is.

—*That's the art of the relation between the center and the periphery.*

Geoffroy de Lagasnerie: If we wanted to be very radical, we could say that the margins can be saved only by the center. Only if we are at the center, only if we have the freedom given by the center and freedom in relation to it, can we carry out actions and provide instruments that can work, when the time comes, for all those who inhabit the margins of the social and intellectual world. To be marginal and pleased to be there often means we take ourselves out of the running so that, politically, we produce nothing. We cancel out the power of our politics if we remain marginal. What Foucault practiced—no doubt he didn't theorize it or even want it, but he practiced it—was the idea that when you are at the center, then you play with the center. That's when you gain effective means for those in the margins of society.

—Isn't that in contradiction with the societal battles that Foucault supported all those years?

Geoffroy de Lagasnerie: Foucault was always very reticent. He never believed in that leftist way of thinking, that populist, workers' credo of being marginal for its own sake. I think he saw the end of politics in that attitude. Power wants people to be marginal for its own sake, since power functions by marginalizing people. His concept of political activity made him oppose movements that marginalized themselves; he wanted to be at the center of thought and the center of institutions, in order to talk about prisons and sexuality at the Collège de France. That's how we destabilize power, instead of fighting as a minority in a ghetto, because ghettoized thought doesn't have an impact. Here I am taking up Didier Eribon in his work *De la subversion.* We find the same remarks in Achille Mbembe's *Critique de la raison nègre.* Both use the same terms to analyze the issue of resistance movements in their relation to the "center." I think that's one of the most important phenomena today, in these times of return to the romanticism of the margins among avant-garde movements. We see how essential intellectual critique is to support social movements, and how indispensable it is to increase their effectiveness.

CONTRIBUTORS

François Caillat is a filmmaker who has directed documentaries for TV and the big screen.

Leo Bersani taught French literature at the University of California (Berkeley). He is the author of *Homos*.

Georges Didi-Huberman is a philosopher and art historian who has worked on the photographic archives of the nineteenth-century Salpêtrière asylum in Paris. His most recent book is *Gerhard Richter: Pictures/Series*.

Arlette Farge is a historian specializing in the eighteenth century; she has written on the history of popular behavior and customs, and the history of male/female relations. She is the author of *The Allure of the Archives*.

Geoffroy de Lagasnerie is a philosopher and sociologist, and a professor in Paris. He is the author of *La dernière leçon de Michel Foucault*.

Paul Rabinow is Professor of Anthropology at the University of California (Berkeley) and an influential writer on the works of Foucault. He is the co-editor of *The Essential Foucault*.

David Homel (translator) is a writer, journalist, filmmaker, and translator. He is the author of seven novels, the most recent being *The Fledglings*. He has translated many French-language books into English, twice receiving the Governor General's Literary Award for Translation. He lives in Montreal.